WASHINGTON BIGFOOT CAMPFIRE STORIES

WASHINGTON BIGFOOT CAMPFIRE STORIES

RUSTY WILSON

Yellow Cat
PUBLISHING™

ISBN: 978-1-948859-29-5

For Jan H.
And for all who love adventure, mystery, and the beautiful
wilderness of the Pacific Northwest

CONTENTS

Foreword ix

Introduction xi

1. An Unusual Evening at Mount Saint Helens 1
2. Lost in the Hoh Rainforest 10
3. The Bigfoot Rustler 22
4. Deadman's Cove 36
5. The Boggy Marsh Monster 47
6. The Gliders 56
7. In the Coulee 67
8. Volcanoes, Goats, and Bigfoot 79
9. Fish and Ships 95
10. The Totem Pole 106
11. Bigfoot, Meet Earthworm 115
12. Hanging Around the Campfire 124

About the Author 131

FOREWORD

Ever thought about exploring the beautiful Evergreen State of Washington? Famous as a Bigfoot Mecca, you'll find not just dramatic scenery, but even more dramatic wildlife.

It's best to know before you go, as they say, and to be prepared. These all new stories (except one) will help you avoid any surprises, well, theoretically at least, for Bigfoot is *always* a surprise.

Fly-fishing guide Rusty Wilson, known as the World's Greatest Bigfoot Storyteller, has spent years collecting these tales from his clients around the campfire over his tasty Dutch-oven dinners, stories guaranteed to make sure you won't want to go out after dark.

Come join a seasoned camper who finds a trail leading to places she doesn't want to go in the Hoh Rainforest in Olympic National Park. Ever wonder what happened to the resident Bigfoot when Mount Saint Helens blew its top? And does Bigfoot rustle cattle? Visit the unique Deadman's Cove just in time to see an unusual sight, as well as finding a real dead man in a marsh all wrapped in ferns—or is it something else? And where did it go?

If these stories don't satisfy your longing for adventure with a twist, keep reading! Watch as strange creatures glide through the remote waterways at Forlorn Lakes, then duck rockslides in one of Washington's coulees.

And what about the pastoral farms near Puyallup? Are they fair game, too? And beautiful Ruby Beach? Is no place sacred? And watch out for totem poles with Bigfoot carved on them, they'll bring nothing but trouble. Be careful when trying to outrun earthworms, and finally, come along on an adventure on a high mountain that nearly ends in tragedy.

You'll want to be sure you're not alone in the woods while reading these stories, and the audio book will keep you entertained as you drive those lonely backroads at night—just don't panic and run off the road!

Another great book from Rusty Wilson, Bigfoot expert and story-teller—tales for both the Bigfoot believer and for those who just enjoy a good story.

———

INTRODUCTION

Greetings, fellow adventurers, to another collection of Bigfoot campfire stories featuring one of our country's most beautiful places —the state of Washington, part of the Pacific Northwest.

For those of you who follow my work, you'll note that it has been some time since I've put together a collection of stories, and some may ask why I saved those from the Bigfoot hotspot of Washington for so long. After all, hasn't the state of Washington been the center of some of the best Bigfoot sightings and stories of all time?

The answer is simple—I've felt overwhelmed by the number of stories I could include, as well as by the strangeness of some of them. Yes, I've heard plenty of odd stories about Bigfoot from other places, but the ones coming from the Pacific Northwest seem to have a quality that no other place can match, and quite frankly, sometimes I have to question their validity. Many of the stories in this collection will provide you with examples of that.

Washington borders huge wilderness areas in Canada, and combined with plenty of wilderness in Oregon and western Montana, it's part of an important habitat for carnivores. Whether Bigfoot should be classified as a carnivore or not remains to be seen, but the region makes great habitat for these large primates, sighted throughout the area since the days the natives hunted and roamed there.

As a flyfishing guide, my home base is in Colorado, and ironically, though the stories happened in Washington, I collected many of them in Colorado, most from around campfires with my flyfishing clients, though some were told to me in private. I'm always very careful to select stories that I believe to be authentic, though how would I ever know without actually being there?

Even though this book has been on the back burner for some time, it's played an important part in how I picture Bigfoot and the many sightings and encounters related to me by my fishing clients. I believe that Washington holds the answers to many of the mysteries that surround the species. As such, I've spent many hours going through my collection of stories to pick the ones I feel best embody the adventure found in that great state.

So, sit back with a cup of hot chocolate in a big comfy chair or by a campfire and enjoy. Get out a map and follow along, and if you ever get the chance to camp or backpack in Washington, be prepared to share your smores with North America's most unique and elusive creature. —Rusty

———

1

AN UNUSUAL EVENING AT MOUNT SAINT HELENS

I don't have a lot of flyfishing clients from Washington, probably because there's plenty of good fishing out there, so no need to come to Colorado. And a lot of my clients are on the younger than 50s side, as the older codger types have figured it out for themselves.

But one particular session found me teaching an older fellow how to fish, and he was from Yakima, Washington. Come to find out, he'd never flyfished before and was eager to learn. His brother was with him, and though most people who fish love solitude, these two stuck together like glue.

One evening around the fire, they told me their story. It took place right before the massive eruption of Mount Saint Helens in 1980. I'll call the pair Hank and Joe, though that's not their real names, and Hank basically told the story.

—Rusty

My brother Joe and I come from a long line of loggers, which is a fairly common profession in Washington with all of the big forests there. We grew up near Mount St. Helens, which, before it blew up, had an extensive logging industry on its foothills and flanks.

In some of the small surrounding towns, most of the citizens were loggers or the families of loggers. That all ended when the mountain blew its top. After that, the only kinds of trees there were dead ones, and the logging industry at the mountain screeched to a halt.

People think of Mount St. Helens and Harry Truman always comes to mind, the old codger who had the lodge up there and refused to leave and of course disappeared. And there is also David Johnston, one of the geologists monitoring the volcano and who called in the famous last words, "Vancouver, Vancouver, this is it!" He was never found, either.

But a number of other people lost their lives up there, too, some of them loggers. All told, the last I heard it was 57 total lives lost. There were also vacationers and locals, and who knows if anyone went missing and wasn't reported because no one knew they were there?

If it hadn't been a Sunday, there would've been lots more lives lost, especially that of loggers, since most of them had gone home for the weekend. The place is now a national monument.

The eruption happened on May 18, 1980, and my brother and I barely missed it. If our dad hadn't decided to go home earlier than planned, we wouldn't be here today, but probably buried in 100 feet of ash. What we saw before the eruption that made him want to leave was pretty amazing, if I don't say so myself.

The mountain gave plenty of warning it was going to blow, and as early as March there were explosions and earthquakes there. It was being closely monitored, and the governor declared a blast zone, but it turned out to be too small. There were barriers and roadblocks set up, but people ignored them and went in anyway.

Spirit Lake on the mountain was very popular for fishing and boating, and it was almost obliterated, though it's come back. There were people on the lake when the mountain blew. Some survived, most didn't.

The landslide of rock and ice from the explosion is considered the largest in the world, and it went over a 1300-foot ridge and on down another 14 miles of the Toutle River. 150 square miles of forest was destroyed. It continued to erupt through 1986, and it's predicted to blow again one of these days.

My dad worked in a logging camp, and because of the state of the mountain, his crew had been told to leave. He was one of the foremen, and he was worried about something happening to their expensive equipment.

My brother and I were just kids, in fourth grade actually, and we were up there with him, which was highly unusual, especially given the danger level. He didn't want to take us up there, but he really felt he had no choice since our mom was in Portland staying with our grandmom, who had just had surgery.

We were supposed to be there just a few days, so I guess he figured it was that or leave us at home to our own devices. Back then, there weren't many rules or regulations, and kids could pretty much do whatever their parents wanted.

We were pretty happy to be skipping school and camping up on the mountain, someplace we usually only got to go when our mom would deliver groceries to Dad. And to be able to sleep in a tent was pretty cool, in our opinion.

So, we got there on a Sunday, and we left on a Saturday, which gave us almost a full week of camping. I will say there was a lot of traffic around for the place being closed, people coming up to see the mountain, as well as geologists and what not, monitoring things.

It was a time I'll never forget, not just because of what we saw, but because it was one of the few times we really got to camp with Dad and spend time with him.

The reason we left on Saturday was partly because my dad's sixth sense told him it was time to get out. I know that sounds odd, but we could clearly see the mountain from where we were, and there was a giant bulge that seemed to be getting bigger and bigger. But there's more to the story of why we left.

How did Dad know to leave that particular day? I don't know, but the eruption happened around nine the next morning, so if we had waited until Sunday to leave, we would've been caught in it, because we wouldn't have gotten out earlier than that.

So we left Saturday evening, and I remember looking up at the mountain before we left and thinking it might be the last time I ever saw it like that. I mentioned this to Joe and he agreed. We were both pretty quiet, as was my dad all the way back down into town.

Years later, Joe and I agreed that the strange things we'd been seeing at night probably had a lot to do with my dad deciding to leave —given what we saw, I'm actually kind of surprised we stuck around as long as we did.

If I were up there now with my kids, I wouldn't have lasted a day. We would be so gone that we wouldn't have even left a trail of dust. But loggers are tough hombres, as was my dad.

So, the day we got up there, the first thing we did was have a big wiener roast. For some reason, hotdogs cooked on a campfire taste really good. If you cook them on the stove or in an oven, they don't even seem like the same thing (I hesitate to even call them food). So, we always had to have a wiener roast when we went camping.

After we got everything set up, we kicked back. It seemed kind of eerie with all the loggers canvas tents still there but nobody around. It was quiet except for a couple of loud booms in the distance. I asked Dad, and he said yes, the mountain was about to erupt, but he thought we had time before it would happen, as it had been booming and spitting out ash since March.

It was pretty spooky, but we finally went to bed. The next day, as Dad was checking on everything, he yelled at us to come over to this tent where he was. We looked inside and something had been there and torn everything up.

There wasn't a lot in there, as the guys had taken their personal stuff back with them, but there were a couple of cots that had been mangled, and the sleeping pads on them had been shredded, as well as the canvas door on the tent.

I remember my dad looking kind of grim and telling us it had to have been a bear, but in retrospect, I know he knew better, he just didn't want us to be scared. (That should tell you something when having a bear in camp is preferable to what actually visited us.)

We spent the rest of the day lounging around, playing some softball and watching the big bulge on the mountain, trying to decide if it had grown any or not, though we didn't hear any more explosions. Along toward evening, we finally decided we wanted another weenie roast.

That was our dinner, and I remember sitting around the fire, feeling kind of conflicted. I was loving being there, but having something tear up a tent, then having heard the mountain boom the evening before had made me realize how precarious our being there really was.

I know we were all pretty quiet that night, and Dad actually asked us if we wanted to go home. We of course said no, because school was still in progress, and it meant we would have to go back.

The next day we went for a drive up to Spirit Lake. I'll never forget how beautiful it was with a deep blue sky and big white puffy clouds and the snowcapped mountain in the distance. Mount St. Helens was called the Mount Fuji of the Pacific Northwest because it was shaped like Mount Fuji, a perfect cone.

Everyone knew it was a dangerous stratovolcano, but I think we were all in denial. The United States didn't have dangerous volcanoes, they were more in places like Asia, Mexico, and Italy. Of course, back then, plate tectonics was still a very new science and people didn't really understand the Ring of Fire like they do now. These stratovolcanoes are created by one plate sliding over another.

OK, so going to Spirit Lake was our second full day at the mountain. We didn't go to the lodge and meet Mr. Truman, and I'm glad we didn't, for it would make it harder to have known him and how he refused to leave, along with his 10 cats. He had a choice, but his cats didn't, and I'm a big cat lover.

That night, things began to get strange. It was probably around two in the morning, when both Joe and I were awakened by something, and I immediately thought it was more explosions on the mountain, but then I realized I could hear something walking around camp.

In a good Bigfoot story, they'll say it sounded like it was on two feet, but I'm actually not really aware of how something on two feet sounds as opposed to four, unless they're walking through leaves or something, and even then I'm not sure I could tell. That's always been puzzling to me about those stories.

But we did hear something, and it was messing around over by some of the logger tents. We were all sleeping in Dad's tent, which was a big heavy canvas army tent that would hold six or eight people. We poked him in the ribs, and told him quietly to get up, but not make any noise. He untied the canvas strings that held the tent door closed, and we all carefully looked out.

The camp was set with a small creek nearby, and we could see what looked like several figures standing down there. They were just standing there, not moving, and another figure was walking around the camp.

It appeared to be trying to look inside the tents, but the doors were all tied close, these old tents not having zippers. Dad grabbed his big light, turned it on and flashed it in the direction where the figure stood, and all heck broke loose.

Quick as a flash, the figure stepped out of the light and around behind the tent, screamed a scream I'll never forget, and the figures down by the creek quickly disappeared.

We were all pretty shaken, because we knew bears didn't travel in groups like that, plus they looked like they were standing up. We didn't get much sleep that night, and the next morning we found footprints down by the creek. They were unbelievable, partly because they were so big and partly because they were barefoot.

Joe and I were scared to death, but Dad seemed pretty pragmatic about it. In retrospect, after living up there as long as he did in logging camps, he knew about Sasquatch. Back then, you never heard anybody talk about them, and if anyone did, they were called Sasquatch. It's almost as if people felt if they didn't acknowledge their existence, they wouldn't be as scary.

Well, Dad told us the figures meant us no harm, and we would stay at least a couple of nights longer. Why he decided this, I'll never know, as we wanted to leave then and there. The fun was over.

That next day, some sheriffs' deputies came by camp and told us we had to leave. Things on the mountain were getting more and more critical, with the geologists' monitors telling them it had to blow soon. I remember Dad telling the deputies we would leave the next morning, even though we ended up staying a couple more days.

To this day. I don't know why we didn't just leave, and my dad's not around any more to explain. Joe thinks he knew it would be the last time he would ever be on the mountain, and we knew he loved that place.

Well, that was a nice day, more beautiful blue skies and good weather, and we heard a few blasts and saw a little bit of steam coming out of the mountain. This was starting to really freak me and Joe out.

We told Dad we wanted to leave, and he said OK, one more night and we would head out. Once again, he didn't seem too worried.

What happened that evening was beyond the pale. We had cooked some hamburgers on the fire, and it was dying out, sparks rising. It wasn't really dark yet, just dusky enough that there were plenty of shadows in the forest, but you could still make things out.

That's when we saw figures coming through the trees across the small meadow where we were camped. There were a half dozen or more, and Dad thought at first it was some fellow loggers that were for some reason having to hike out of their camp.

I remember him commenting that they could ride in the back of his pickup on the way down, so it wouldn't be a problem. The group stopped at the creek and drank, bending down onto their knees, which we found really odd, since they were almost in our camp, and surely we would have water or at least something to drink from.

When they stood back up, the light from the last sunrays cut across a couple of the taller ones to where we could make them out better. We could easily see that they were not human.

Joe and I have talked about this many times, trying to describe them, but the light was such that we didn't see a lot of detail. But they were big, covered with long hair, especially hanging off their arms, and basically just looked like large upright apes, and we could see a couple of them were carrying what looked like large walking sticks.

Now the creatures stood by the creek, motionless, as if they'd just noticed us. But instead of running and hiding like the one we'd seen messing around the tent, they then started walking right through our camp. That's when we could see them close enough to be certain of what we were seeing—these were definitely not people.

We watched them until they were out of sight over a distant ridge and it got too dark to see anything. They left a chill behind them, not because we felt like they wanted to harm us, but because it seemed like we'd had a group hallucination. How could something like this even exist?

Later, back in town when we weren't so scared and could talk a little more freely about it, Dad told us that he and his fellow loggers had seen these creatures around ever since they'd first started working on the mountain. They'd logged at plenty of other places and never seen them, but there was something about the Mount St. Helens area that seem to attract them, and they didn't seem to be very afraid of people.

Well, Joe and I didn't really want to go into the tent because we felt vulnerable in there, as we couldn't see what was going on, so we ended up sitting by the fire until probably about 3 a.m. The big dipper at that point had turned upside down, and now we could hear more explosions coming from the mountain. Dad was in the tent sleeping like a baby, even though several times during the night we heard more footsteps going through camp.

That next morning, we got up and found tracks heading straight for a big ridge behind us. I counted what looked like 20 or 30, all going through our camp. Who knows how many went around?

Dad was pretty quiet as we loaded up our tent and all of our stuff, and he then decided to take a couple of other tents down, and we ended up filling up the back of our truck, along with some camping gear that belonged to the logging camp. If we hadn't taken that stuff, it would now be buried under ash. He gave it back to the logging company, who was glad to have it, especially since at that point they'd lost all their expensive heavy equipment from the eruption.

Joe and I have gone back several times to where we thought the camp sat, and nothing looks the same. Even the creek has a different path, and some of the little ridges and hills that we hiked up were completely gone.

We got down off the mountain by mid-afternoon, and when we pulled into our driveway, we were dirty and exhausted to the point that we didn't even unload anything, but went straight into the house, took showers, and dad cooked up some stuff from the freezer that mom had left. If I remember right, we had spaghetti and meatballs for dinner. It's funny what one remembers.

The next morning, Joe and I were out in the yard unloading the truck and as I turned, my jaw hit the floor. A huge ash cloud billowed up into the sky. We were a good 40 miles from the mountain and yet had ash coming down on everything for days. My aunt, who lived in Colorado, said they even had ash on their cars there. Ash covered everything and everybody for a long time and I heard some enterprising kids were selling jars of it to travelers.

Mom came back a few days later. Grandmother had recovered nicely and was home in Portland with Grandpa, and we would all end up going over there to stay with them for part of the summer on their small farm out in the country. With time, our week on Mount St. Helens started feeling surreal, like a dream. Nobody really talked about it for a long time.

It was just so far from the realm of our experience that it's almost like we wanted it to just go away. We've gone back to the mountain a number of times, but I refuse to camp there, and I know Joe feels the same.

And every time I look at the mountain, which is now just a shell of what it once was with its caved-in top, I think of all those Sasquatch and how they knew it was time to go.

———

2

LOST IN THE HOH RAINFOREST

I met Mia while guiding a group kind of like Sisters on the Fly, outdoorsy women who wanted to learn to flyfish. We had a great time fishing the Roaring Fork River near Glenwood Springs, Colorado, and they invited me to a potluck dinner they were having at their campground.

Since I usually provide a Dutch-oven dinner as part of my guided trips, it was a real treat to not have to cook. Mia's story was one I can identify with, having spent time in Olympic National Park.

—Rusty

My name is Mia. I've never believed in Bigfoot, thinking it was just folklore, though it always kind of fit in the horror category for me. I have a couple of friends who love horror movies, which is something I can't watch. I remember asking them why they liked them, and they said because it made them feel alive.

Well, when I see scary movies, I certainly do feel alive, but I also worry about dying from fear. I just don't have the disposition for that kind of stuff, so I always avoid it. But the scariest thing I've ever seen outdoes any scary movie my friends have seen.

Having said that, I'm the opposite when I'm outdoors, because almost nothing scares me—or I should say, *used* to scare me. Maybe it's because I grew up with active parents, and we did a lot of camping and hiking. Hiking alone didn't used to bother me, and I loved the solitude and quiet.

My friends never understood this. They would worry about every little sound, assuming I could even get them to go with me. I really think seeing all these horror movies contributed to their imaginations going off-track.

I think people tend to be afraid of what they don't understand. This is the basis for most superstitions, in my opinion, as well as what's behind a lot of prejudices. It used to seem kind of ironic to me that people would come up with scary explanations for the unknown, but now I understand why, as the unknown can be very scary.

At the time this happened, I lived in Olympia, which is the capital of Washington. I had just finished school and had managed to get a pretty good job working as a teacher in nearby Tumwater, which gave me the summers off.

I'm originally from Illinois, and I went to Olympia on a scholarship at Evergreen State. I was happy to be there, as I loved the rainforest and the ocean and everything about the area, it was so different from Illinois. Now, I'm not so sure.

I was ecstatic when summer came around after my first year of teaching, because I now had my freedom and could start getting out and doing some serious hiking. I had tons of books on the flora and fauna of that part of the state, as I was really into identifying plants and trees and mushrooms and that kind of thing. I was fascinated by what they call the temperate rainforest. I started going out to Olympic National Park and hiking the trails there.

If you've never been to the Olympic Peninsula, you're in for a real treat, assuming you like vegetation—and I will add that you might be in for something else, if you're not careful.

It's a really rainy place, and the part of the park called the Hoh Rainforest gets around 140 inches of rain each year. It's named after the Hoh River, whose name comes from a native language.

All this water results in a paradise for plants, with lots of lush mosses and ferns growing under a canopy of huge trees—and most of it is never visited by humans. It's just a morass of greenery, a magical fairyland, with spruce and pine trees with moss hanging from the branches and dense ferns carpeting the ground.

When I first discovered Olympic National Park, I was enthralled. There's a campground there called the Hoh Rainforest Campground, and I pitched my tent in Loop C, down by the river. I spent several days exploring, watching the river otters, meeting fellow campers, and generally having a great time. Like I said, I love being outdoors, and I even wondered if I could get a job there as a camp host.

I was soon exploring the trails, noting that the farther you get from camp, the thinner the crowds get. If you go far enough and step off into the woods (assuming you can, it's so thick), the silence becomes mystical. You feel like you could be an old tree, with the other trees talking to you in the breeze.

I discovered it was a great place to meditate. I'm not into serious meditation techniques, I mostly just like to sit and think. I'll never forget the first time I stopped to sit in the trees—an elk came walking down the trail, stopped only a few feet away and stood watching me, then peacefully walked off into the wilderness.

I ended up almost moving into the forest. You can stay in a campground for two weeks, then you have to relocate. I would go home every two weeks for a few days and re-supply and shower and all that, then go back out.

There are a number of campgrounds in Olympic National Park, so I was always able to find a spot for another two weeks. I might add that this was before the parks got so popular and you had to have reservations.

But even though I still love the rainforest and cherish my time there, I had warnings and red flags that I chose to ignore, primarily because I had no fears nor worries about what was out there. I knew there were bears and probably mountain lions, but I had never seen or heard anything about them, other than in my nature books.

But every once in awhile, and thinking back, this wasn't only in the Hoh Campground, I would have something odd occur. It was a variety of things, and at the time they didn't seem to have any connections, but looking back, I can see a pattern was emerging.

For example, my first week out there, it was late evening, and I was sitting in a camp chair outside my tent when I heard a strange howling sound coming from far in the distance. I wasn't the only one who heard it, and a lot of campers started talking about it. A couple of people even walked over by my camp to listen, because I was the one closest to the forest.

I talked with them for awhile, and we all decided it had to be a mountain lion. I do remember it being really odd and making me feel uncomfortable, but I was quickly over it, enthralled by being there.

Nothing unusual happened after that for some time, but I do recall several times seeing what looked like people at the edge of the forest, except they were all wispy and wavy and would quickly disappear. It wasn't just me, this was also something other people noticed. I remember talking to a couple and we all decided it was mist and fog. The rainforest was like that, mysterious.

Another time, I heard something huge crashing through the forest when I was way out on the trail, and it struck me as odd because it didn't sound anything like an elk or deer, which I would run into quite frequently. It sounded much larger and like maybe it was on two legs. But like I said, I wasn't afraid when I was hiking, and that was just a one-time thing for me.

There was a time when I was out sitting on a log a little off trail when I heard what sounded like a deep guttural growl. That really spooked me, and I went straight back to camp. I remember not going back out very far after that for a couple of weeks, but I then decided it was a bear or lion and would be long gone, so I started going back out.

And of course, the longer I stayed there, the more comfortable I got. I did stay in other campgrounds because of the two-week thing, but the Hoh Campground was my favorite. I got to know the trails there really well. This was all a prelude to what ended my summer explorations, and I eventually left Washington.

I remember one morning when several people took down their tents and were preparing to leave, all in spots near me. I just happened by on my way to the restrooms when I stopped and asked why they were leaving. We had talked the night before, and they'd said they were staying a week.

Something really strange had scared them during the night, and they didn't plan on coming back. They really didn't want to talk but just told me I should leave. I did manage to get out of them that something had messed around their tents and one of them had seen a huge creature with glowing eyes.

If they hadn't been so frightened, I would've laughed it off, thinking it was just an elk and they'd probably watched too many horror movies or what not. Like I said, I don't like horror movies, and the power of suggestion can be very real, especially when you're out in the wilderness. I thought about it for awhile, but after they left, camp seemed quiet and normal. I felt like I was in paradise, a place I could stay forever.

One day, I found a small clearing that you could just barely see from the trail, and I made my way through the undergrowth out to it. It looked like someone had torn out the brush, and in retrospect, I should've found this highly suspicious, but I just figured it was the work of the guys that maintained the trail. Maybe they had created a spot where they could take a break.

I sat there for several hours, lost in the peace and quiet, just thinking about life and all the stuff one thinks about when it's quiet like that. I'm kind of a thinker more than a doer, I guess. I then headed back to camp and built a nice fire and ate dinner.

The next day, I had new neighbors in camp next to me, a nice couple from Eugene, Oregon, and they invited me over for tacos, which was nice. I get that a lot because I'm single and I guess people feel sorry for me, which I find kind of ironic, because I love being alone—but I also sometimes enjoy conversation.

I later realized that talking to them helped save my life, because they knew how long I was planning to stay and noticed there was no one in my camp.

I should mention that all the trailheads for this area are located at the end of the Upper Hoh Road, next to the Hoh Rainforest Visitor Center, the opposite direction from the campground. Two short loop trails start nearby (the Hall of Mosses and the Spruce Nature Trail) as well as a longer trail (the Hoh River Trail).

The Hall of Mosses Trail and the Spruce Nature Trail are short, being a little less than two miles long, but the Hoh River Trail goes 17 miles to a camping area called Glacier Meadows, then ends 18.5 miles at the Blue Glacier Moraine under Mt. Olympus. Another trail, the Hoh Lake Trail, goes to Bogachiel Peak between the Hoh and the Sol Duc Valley. I mention this because the trail provides access into some deep wilderness, and it's my belief that other creatures besides humans and general wildlife use the trails.

Well, it was on one of the two shorter trails that I found the little clearing, which made it easy to get to. I was going there every day, enjoying hanging out, until one day when I guess I must've woken up to the red flags, because all of a sudden the place felt creepy.

I was puzzled. Why did a place that had felt so familiar and special now feel strange? I looked around a little closer. The clearing had definitely been made by someone—I figured whoever maintained the trail—but I now looked closer at where vegetation had been taken out.

The trees had been broken off, not cut with a saw, just wrenched out of the ground and thrown into the nearby bushes. One was a good two feet in diameter, a red cedar, and it had been pulled up by its roots.

Another was a tall Sitka spruce, and it had been broken off at its base, leaving jagged pieces of trunk sticking up. And the log I'd been using as a chair was actually a Douglas fir, a good 20 feet tall, also broken off at its base. Shrubs and plants had also been wrenched out of the ground.

What could have done such damage? I couldn't figure it out. Trail workers would've cut the trees down, not pushed them over or pulled them up by their roots. And why clear out a place so near the visitor center? They could just go there instead for lunch or to kick back.

None of it made sense, and I then noticed a complete absence of birds in the area. Normally, the rainforest had tons of robins and Canada Grey Jays, but I saw nary a bird. I finally decided it was the weather that was keeping them away—maybe they were hiding out from an incoming storm, but I knew this couldn't be it, as I'd never seen birds there.

Whatever it was, I decided I no longer wanted to be there, so I went back to my camp. Actually, I went to the visitor center first, just to be around people, something out of the norm for me. I felt insecure and threatened, yet I had no idea why.

That night the dreams began. I can't really describe them other than to say they were kind of like those misty people at the edge of the forest—undefined and strange and otherworldly. I couldn't even tell you what they were about, they were so impressionistic. They left me feeling unsettled all the next day, as well as sleep-deprived and tired.

I spent all that day in camp, reading and hanging out. I actually even contemplated going home, though I still had plenty of supplies and there was no real reason not to stay. I finally went over to my neighbors' camp and hung out for awhile, which made me feel better, as they were a cheerful and upbeat couple.

That night, I slept really well and woke up feeling refreshed. I had no idea what the previous night had been about, but I decided maybe I was catching a bug or something. Whatever it was, I had kicked it and was raring to go.

I was soon back on the trail, but this time I packed to spend all day with some extra food and water and my rain jacket, which I always carried. But for some reason I had also stuffed my down vest into my pack, probably because it was a bit chilly that morning.

I was soon at the visitor center and heading up the Hoh River Trail. It was a beautiful day, though the forest was misty and foggy. I met various people along the trail, some backpacking to Glacier Meadows. I didn't envy them carrying their heavy packs. I felt happy and carefree, back to my normal state, the fears and weirdness forgotten.

But I did miss my meditation spot—I missed being able to slip off the trail and be in the beautiful small clearing, surrounded by tall Sitka spruce and Douglas fir, with giant ferns everywhere. It was starting to feel like I could almost talk to the trees.

Surely there were other places like that where I could slip off the trail and not be seen. I decided to keep an eye open, and before I knew it, I had found a small game trail that took off from the main trail. I decided to follow it for a short distance. I could turn around and walk back to the main trail at any time.

The trail immediately curved a little and went down into a small ravine, where the vegetation was even thicker than before, if one could imagine that. I soon came upon a small area that had a nice log I could sit on. Everything looked totally normal, the result of jumbled rocks that had been carried by water into the ravine.

I sat for awhile, thinking about everything, when fragments from the dream of that unsettled night came back to me. I hadn't been able to remember the dreams before, but now I could clearly see figures floating in and out of deep forests, following me wherever I went. I was unable to get rid of them, and they suddenly felt real.

I stood, feeling panicked, like I needed to get back on the main trail. That panic is what led me astray, for I wasn't thinking clearly. It felt like the misty figures were after me, and I took off half-running.

I was still on the game trail when I realized what I was doing and stopped. I was puffing and panting, and I stood for awhile, trying to catch my breath, half afraid to look behind me. When I did, there was of course nothing there.

I knew I had run the wrong way down the trail, so I turned around and started back. When you don't have anything to navigate by except forest and trees, it's easy to lose your sense of direction, which I apparently did.

I backtracked on the trail to where I had been, but now everything looked different. The log I'd been sitting on seemed to have more moss on it, and I wasn't even sure it was the same one. I started back down what I thought was the right path, only to have it veer and head up the other side of the ravine, and I hoped that if I went up it, I'd be where the main Hoh River Trail was.

I must've backtracked on three or four different game trails by the time I realized I was totally lost. Because the vegetation is so hard to navigate, the rainforest has a lot of game trails, and it's easy to get lost. I had nothing to orient myself by, and I realized I was walking in circles when I went by the same log the second time.

It occurred to me to stay put and see if I could get someone's attention, so I started yelling. It finally dawned on me to check my phone for a signal, but of course there wasn't one. I was a long way from the nearest cell tower.

I sat on a different log, this time trying to center myself and gather my wits. I ate some nuts and drank some water, then tried some deep breathing exercises. Getting lost out in the desert or mountains isn't much fun, but at least you have landmarks and places you can climb to and look out. I had neither, and everything looked the same.

I finally decided that if I followed the ravine downstream it would eventually come out at some kind of waterway, maybe even the Hoh River, since water flows downhill. I started out, but didn't get very far in the tangled mass.

The problem with the rainforest is that it's so thick there's no place you can go except on game trails, unless you have a machete. I walked back the other way along the ridge, hoping to hear the sound of the river, but there was nothing.

OK, it was now getting to be late afternoon, and I knew I needed to figure something out soon. There was no way I wanted to spend the night out there, and who was to say I would be able to find my way back the next day? If I couldn't find my way back now, what would be different?

This is where my friendliness with my neighbors back at the campground was returned to me in spades, for that night, when they realized I hadn't come back to camp, they notified a ranger and a search party was put together, even though they couldn't search after dark. But of course I didn't know this. I ended up spending the night and the entire next day out there, lost.

I will never forget being alone out in the middle of the misty rain-forest at night, and I was so glad I'd stuck my down vest in my pack because it was the only thing that kept me from freezing. It wasn't terribly cold, but hypothermia is a real danger once it gets below 55 degrees. Having that down vest with my rainproof coat over it was the only thing that kept me dry and warm.

I know I slept because when I woke, the forest was light enough to make out the shapes of the trees. I was extremely uncomfortable but had managed to sleep anyway, and when I woke up I wanted really badly to stretch out, but something told me to freeze and stay still.

That's when I saw it. There was a shape shadow not far away standing in the middle of the trail. It was large, and I suspected it had to be an elk because of its size. Yet something told me I was in danger, so I didn't move an inch.

I watched as the shadow walked up the trail, then sat down, just like a human would, like it had arms and legs and a torso. I was terri-fied. This was no deer or elk. What was it? Had it seen me?

It sat there until the sun came up enough that I could make out some details. I couldn't believe my eyes. Was I looking at a Bigfoot? It looked just like other people have described it—big, with long hair all over, muscular arms and legs, and a large head. It was backlit in the rising sun, making its fur shine a golden brown. I couldn't really make out its face, and it didn't seem to have much of a neck, its head just melting into thick massive shoulders.

For some reason I got the feeling it was a male, probably because of its muscular size. It was holding a big stick, almost as tall as it was. I was still scared, but the feeling of impending doom had lifted, and I now felt like I was in the presence of an intelligent creature. Did it intend to harm me? The longer we both sat there, the more I decided it didn't. Maybe it was just curious, like I was.

I finally said in a quiet voice, "I'm lost. Can you help me?"

It stood and was immediately joined by two wispy beings. Where they came from, I don't know, they appeared so quickly. It's hard to describe, but it was like you could put your hand through them. And, of course, it was still foggy and misty, so they kind of blended in with the trees.

Rusty, I don't keep up with the Bigfoot world like you do, but I'm wondering if anyone has ever postulated a connection between Bigfoot and—I'm not sure what to call it—the spirit world maybe? It sounds totally ludicrous, or maybe there are some kind of beings that live in the Olympic rainforest that look like ghosts.

I later wondered if the fog hadn't played a trick on my eyes and made them look ethereal when they were actually real people. Whatever they were, they stood there looking at me with big circular eyes. They didn't seem to be talking to each other or anything. They made me extremely uncomfortable.

Finally, they left. I can't say which direction they went, they just seemed to melt into the fog. The Bigfoot was still holding the big stick, and it eventually turned and went back down the trail, dragging it along next to it. It was really odd.

I was suspecting at that point that I was hallucinating. I remember thinking this was nothing at all like I thought losing one's mind would be, but something had to explain all this strangeness.

What was interesting was that not more than an hour or two after these beings and the Bigfoot left, the search and rescue party found me. They had apparently been following my tracks and knew I was in the area.

In retrospect, I was no worse for the wear, because I had enough food and water that I wasn't hurting any, and because I had my down vest I'd managed to stave off hypothermia by staying warm and dry. I was able to walk back out with the rescue party, everyone in good spirits. I was quite a ways off the Hoh River Trail, and to this day I have no idea how I got so lost.

Once back at the campground, I went to the couple next to my camp and thanked them. If it wasn't for them, I would probably still be out there, although, surely the camp host would've noticed I was overstaying my reservation and called a ranger. But I had another 10 days to go, and by then I would probably have been history.

I spent the night in my tent, too tired to pack up and go home.

The next day I took everything down and headed out. I decided to stop at the visitor center to tell them I was leaving my camp early so someone else could reserve it.

What was interesting was that I came upon one of the rangers who had been part of the search party, and we had a nice long talk. He told me I wasn't the first person to get lost out there, and I was pretty lucky, because the deep rainforest isn't very forgiving, and a number of people had just simply disappeared.

What kind of blew my mind, though, was how they'd known where to look for me. He said they'd found a path where someone had been dragging a stick, and they figured it was me. Bears and other animals don't drag sticks along.

I didn't have the heart to say what it was, but I later wished I had, because I bet he himself had a few stories to tell. Maybe we could've compared notes. I later heard a number of stories from the Hoh Rainforest and the Olympic Peninsula, and it's actually a Bigfoot hotbed.

I've since moved back to Illinois to be closer to my family. I have a sister who has kids, and they want me to take a few weeks this coming summer to go visit Washington with them. I told them I'd go, but I won't go hiking on the trails.

Maybe someday I'll tell them why.

3

THE BIGFOOT RUSTLER

Most of my stories come from flyfishing clients, but occasionally I will meet people and we get to talking and one thing leads to another and we're talking about Bigfoot. In this case, I met Ricky and his brother, Wyatt, in the small mountain town of Skykomish, where the pair were eating lunch under a Bigfoot statue at an espresso place. They had a really cute stock dog with them who they said was named Chester, or Chet.

I made a comment about the statue, which started a fascinating conversation. People ask me if these stories are true or not, and all I have to go by is my own judgment when I hear them, but something about this pair made me pretty certain they were telling the truth. I'll never know for sure, but their stories matched perfectly, and they both still seemed visibly shaken by what had happened.

Sometimes I will reveal where an encounter took place, but in this case, I think it's better not to, since the house is still there with people living in it, and it's so easily accessible, being right by the highway. I know what they told me gave me pause, and I doubt if I'll ever stop along this particular stretch of highway. And I might forewarn you that this is one of the stranger Bigfoot stories I've ever heard. Wyatt did the majority of the telling so I'll leave it in his voice.

—Rusty

. . .

Rusty, we don't tell this story to just anyone, and I hope you don't come out the other side of this thinking we're totally nuts, but if you do I guess that's just how it is. I don't know, maybe we are—totally nuts, that is.

We're both fourth-generation Washingtonians. That means our great-grandparents settled here. Four generations doesn't sound like much, but what makes it interesting is that we all lived on the same piece of land that my great-grandparents settled.

My parents broke that tie by selling it, but I don't think any of the family would have complained about that, seeing what happened there.

Our property had a small barn and some corrals and 40 acres of nice hayfields that went with it. It was pretty much surrounded by forest, on the lower flanks of the Cascades, some of the last open land before going over a major pass. Our dad kept a few dairy cows when we were kids, so Ricky and I were used to being around livestock, which is what led to the rest of the story, as they say.

What started all this was when we were in high school and went to a rodeo in a nearby town. We of course thought we were country boys, more knowledgeable than most, and when we saw the bull riding we decided that's what we wanted to do. It was exciting and had enough danger that we could impress the girls, plus it paid really well if you did manage to win anything. The flip side was you could spend all your earnings and then some in the emergency room.

The first thing we did was go home and try to ride our milk cows, which was a disaster. We quickly realized we didn't have the equipment to be a bull-riding facility, so we then built a small chute with a corral leading into it where we could push the bulls and get them ready for the ride, assuming we ever got any bulls.

In the meantime, we hung out as much as possible at some of the nearby rodeos trying to learn what we could about bull riding. Back then hardly anyone was doing it, just some of the more hard-core cowboys that rode the circuit. Everyone else was like us, they didn't have any way to get into it or practice. It wasn't nearly as popular as it is now, where you can actually go to ranch camps to learn how to ride.

To make a long story short, we managed to set up a riding area and buy a couple of young bulls. My dad wasn't real happy about our enterprise, though I think he found it entertaining.

It didn't take long for these two young bulls to catch on to what we were up to. They got to where they wouldn't buck at all. We would get on them and they would stop and just stand there and look at us. We finally realized you have to put a cinch around their flanks, but after awhile, even that stopped working.

That's when we found out the rodeo bulls were from special breeding stock that was bred to be what they called rank bulls, bucking and disliking people on their backs, though some of the most famous and rankest bulls are actually very gentle until you get on them.

I don't remember what we did with the bulls, except I know we sold them and bought another pair that was supposedly rodeo stock. It wasn't long until we had the same result—bored bulls. So much for our bull-riding enterprise.

I forgot to mention that Ricky also ended up with a broken rib where he got kicked, and we found out that serious injuries were just par for the course in bull riding.

It was about then that a puppy we ended up naming Chester showed up, someone having dumped him by the highway, or so we figured, as we weren't able to find his owners, and he didn't have an ID. He was a Blue Heeler, the perfect breed of dog for cattle ranching.

We found out several months later that he'd jumped out of the cab of our neighbor's pickup while they were talking to our folks, and nobody had noticed. I think that was the only neighbor we didn't contact about him. He ended up letting us keep him.

It was about then that my dad said we needed to start contributing to the family income, since we'd both graduated high school. I think this was part of his plan to dissuade us from bull riding and get us out into the real world.

Well, we made lousy bull riders, so why not be stock contractors? They made lots of money, and the only risks they had were dealing with the animals, loading and unloading, that kind of thing, but no riding. We decided to work with our bulls and train them to be wild. Can you guess we knew very little about livestock? Once we'd trained them, we could lease them out to rodeos.

Those two bulls we bought ended up getting pretty big. They were part brahma, which is what a lot of the rodeo stock is descended from these days. As for training them to be wild, all we needed was a pair of spurs, and we had some wild bulls. They hated us after that and would even go after us when we were in the corral, so we learned a little bullfighting, too. Chester, who we now called Chet, learned to bite their heels, making them even madder.

Bullfighting is what used to be the job of the rodeo clowns, who would make sure the bulls didn't get to the riders after getting bucked off. Bullfighting is now a sport of its own, and I'm not talking about the kind in Spain, but rather getting a bull to chase you instead of the rider. There are bullfighting competitions, and the bull never gets hurt. If anyone does, it's the bullfighter. Chet was a good bullfighter, and fortunately, never got hurt.

We finally got our bulls to a small rodeo, where they did well, and we made a bit of cash, maybe enough to feed them for a month, but better than nothing. We bragged about that to our parents, but they weren't that impressed.

Keep in mind that a good bull can make hundreds of thousands of dollars any more on the rodeo circuit. There are bulls who have made it possible for their owners to purchase entire ranches. When I say that I'm thinking of top notch stock like Bodacious and Man Hater, the bulls that make it to the National Bull-Riding Finals.

So, how does all this fit into a Bigfoot or Sasquatch story? Stay tuned.

So, we were now on our way to becoming stock contractors. We used our dad's old pickup and stock trailer to haul the bulls, and ended up taking them to a dozen rodeos that summer. Chet ended up being a valuable part of our team, helping us load and unload by biting at their heels.

Now, even though we were close to the wilds with our small ranch, there was a ranch nearby that was right on the edge of wilderness and an actual working cattle ranch with pretty large herds. The cowboys would push the cattle up into the mountains in the spring, where the cattle would feed on forest service land until fall, then they would bring them back down.

This ranch had been around since the late 1800s and was generally pretty well run. I don't know how many cattle they had, even though our parents were friends with the owners.

Well, one afternoon one of the owners came by the house and told us they'd been missing cattle recently and asked us to keep an eye out for them. It wasn't a large number, maybe less than a dozen, but it was unusual for cattle to go missing. It seems like they were wondering if there wasn't somebody rustling them.

Ricky and I weren't too concerned about rustlers, because at that point our bulls were getting kind of hard to handle. Our so-called training was actually turning them into problems. If someone tried to rustle them, they were probably going to get hurt.

We were sitting around in the backyard of the house one evening, trying to decide what to name our new enterprise—should we go with R&A Stock Contracting or A&R? My dad was there, smoking his pipe, and suggested we call ourselves Two-Bull Stock Contractors, which he said was better than No-Bull Stock Contractors. He was once again being entertained by what he thought was our lack of business sense.

Ricky and I tried to be patient, but we finally told him how much money we'd made, which was a big mistake. We'd already shared our earnings with Mom, but he hit the roof, saying we needed to put some of it back into the business and buy more stock, which surprised us.

But what surprised us even more was the strange sound that came from deep in the forest behind us. It sounded like a deep gong, like in some movie about Tibet, the sound going out in waves that didn't seem to dissipate like a normal sound wave would but to just disappear into the forest. It's really hard to explain, but it also had a strange resonance to it.

Imagine someone hitting a gong and then as the gong reverberated it sounded more and more like an animal or person, kind of going woa woa woa. Whatever it was, it was way back in there, and we could hear the sound coming for quite some time.

Our dad is very pragmatic, yet I could see he was visibly startled by it, and he said it had to be a truck going up the nearby mountain pass. Ricky and I just looked at each other in shock, for it wasn't any sound either of us had ever heard. When it sounded a second time I felt a chill go through me and immediately wanted to go inside.

As we were walking toward the house, I could see our two bulls were also affected by it. They actually tried to push through the gate and ended up hunched over in the corner of the corral.

"That was weird," I said as we stood in the kitchen looking out the window. It was then that our mom told us all about having heard it several times in the previous few days. It had freaked her out enough that she wasn't going out in the backyard. She didn't tell us about it because we were gone.

That night, as Ricky and I were feeding the bulls, we heard it again, except it sounded closer. It wasn't nearly as tinny sounding, and you could tell it was made by something huge. We both agreed that there was no way it was a truck going up the pass, but we had no idea what it was.

The bulls wouldn't relax enough to eat and ended up over in the corner of the corral. I went out again just before bedtime and they were still standing there, their hay untouched. When they saw me, they came over as if wanting to be near me, which was an odd feeling, as we usually avoided each other.

They were big and half-wild and scary and would even sometimes try to hook me with their horns. But now they were as docile as puppies. We're talking animals that weighed a good 1600 pounds each. They even tried to nose Chet instead of kicking at him.

Ricky's always been pretty much on the same wavelength as me, and I wasn't surprised when he came out to the corral. We decided to hang out there and see if we could coax the bulls to eat. It seemed that all they could think about was going into the barn, so we let them go in. When we brought their hay inside, they started eating.

Ricky and I were getting ready to go back into the house, as the bulls seemed to have settled down and had eaten quite a bit of hay. We decided to just leave them in the barn all night and close up the doors. But as we were walking out, we heard that strange noise again, except now it was very close.

The bulls immediately ran into the far corner of the barn, as if trying to hide. Ricky quickly pulled the barn door closed and latched it, and then he and I made a beeline for the haymow part of the barn, where we startled a couple of mice that ran for the exits.

I don't know why we thought being up there would be particularly safe, but it felt like the only place we could go, and the bulls were right below us, which we hoped would add some protection. Chet is really agile and ended up climbing the ladder to be with us.

We kind of burrowed down into the hay, Chet in the middle, and Ricky next to a crack in the wall, where he could see out, so he kept a lookout. It wasn't long until he said he could see a strange blue light coming from the forest and heading toward the barn. It really freaked him out.

When he told me it had stopped just outside the barn door, he whispered that he couldn't tell what it was, if it was a person or something else, just a glowing blue light. At that point the bulls were just totally beyond freaked out. They actually tried to get into the tack room, which was way too small for them and was closed up anyway.

So we just waited and waited to see what would happen. It wasn't long until I had the strangest feeling, something like I was drifting along some river somewhere far away with no concern for anything. It was kind of like a loss of one's agency or one's ability to be self-directed. I was like a piece of wood floating on the river. I later asked Ricky about it, and he said he felt the same way.

And while this strange feeling was over us, we could see the blue light glowing at the front of the barn, and Ricky looked out the crack and said that there were a couple more standing over in the edge of the forest. At that point we were so out of it we weren't afraid.

You know how a throbbing goes through everything when a car goes by that has their bass turned up really loud? It just occurred to me that the sound we heard was a lot like that.

I don't know how long we were out there, but I do know we both fell asleep or passed out or something. When I woke up, both of the bulls were sleeping, kind of out of it just like me and Ricky.

Ricky and I eventually went inside and tried to figure out what had happened, but we were so tired we ended up going to bed. The next day, everything was back to normal and the bulls seemed fine.

As we talked about it over breakfast, we wondered if there hadn't somehow accidentally been some kind of carbon monoxide leak or something, as it was just too bizarre. Our parents didn't even miss us while we were in the barn, even though it was dark, which is not at all like them. They usually kept an eye on things with these bulls around.

Later, Ricky and I talked about this some more, and we both had a very strong feeling that the reason whatever it was came around was that it sensed some kind of energy or something that was around the bulls. It really felt like that, and I can't even describe why, but it was like it was on its way through and somehow could feel the energy.

It took us several days to feel normal. It was like we'd had the flu or a cold or something—we were functioning, but not thinking with any acuity at all. It was like being at a high altitude without a lot of oxygen.

Finally, that evening, we got together with Mom and Dad in the living room and tried to piece together what had happened. Mom didn't even want to talk about it, but she did sit and listen and finally agreed that something strange was going on.

Well, the peace and quiet didn't last long because that same night I heard the sound in the distance and went and got Ricky, and the first thing we did was take the bulls and put them in the barn with plenty of hay. We locked everything up and went back inside the house. We didn't want to be out there again like last time. We then sat in the living room with the curtains open a crack and watched.

Sure enough, before long a strange blue light hovered around the barn and another one or two were over on the edge of the forest, but we still couldn't make out what they were. Finally, Ricky said, "Wyatt, they've broken into the barn. The blue light is inside." We both agreed that it felt very ominous.

It was then that I heard the strangest rumbling sounds, and I later figured out it was the bulls, who were terrified. I wanted to go out and do something to rescue them. I grabbed my shotgun, but Ricky wouldn't let me go, saying that it was something beyond our knowledge. Mom and Dad were still up and around and agreed with Ricky that we had to stay inside, and it wasn't long before the lights were gone and everything was quiet.

I wanted to go out then, but to be honest with you I was scared stiff, so we waited until dawn. Nobody got any sleep.

We went out to the barn and to our surprise, the bulls were totally gone. The barn door was wide open, and there were no signs of any kind of struggle. It looked like the bulls just walked right out. The only thing of note was an odd smell, kind of like when you solder something or have an electrical short.

Because we lived on the flanks of the Cascades, we got lots of rain, and more often than not the ground around the ranch was somewhat muddy. We decided to try to track the bulls, but when we saw what we were dealing with, we knew we needed to go back and prepare ourselves better.

What were we dealing with? Ricky had found several footprints that were the equivalent of about four or five of ours together. Each print had toes, which meant we weren't dealing with someone wearing shoes, which made whatever it was even larger than we'd thought. Neither of us believed in Bigfoot, but we'd heard lots of stories, especially living in Washington. Even so, it seemed ludicrous to us that a Bigfoot would come and steal our cattle, especially a Bigfoot lit up with blue lights. It didn't make sense to me.

Well, Ricky thought it did make sense because Bigfoot had to eat something, so why not beef? I argued that they would go for something easier to deal with than our two bulls, but he said the bulls were so docile from fear that they probably walked off with them like puppy dogs.

I still wasn't sure I believed in Bigfoot, but I was willing to let the bulls go their way rather than meet up with one. Ricky was pretty adamant about searching for them. He said that maybe the bulls had gotten away from the Bigfoot, and we could find them somehow. He then made a case that Bigfoot had to have something to eat in the winter, so maybe they were taking cattle, like herders. I told him this was ridiculous.

So, we got our packs ready with some food and water and rifles. We put more ammo in those packs than we'd gone through in several years just target practicing. Mom tried to talk us out of it, and Dad again seemed to find it vaguely entertaining. He didn't act too worried about anything.

It was later, when talking to him after it was all over, that he revealed he'd had his own Bigfoot encounter years before. Apparently he'd come across one while out horseback riding, but it hadn't done anything, and he found it more interesting than frightening. He never believed they were particularly dangerous. He said he had no idea that's what we were dealing with because of the blue light, which was all new to him.

I guess Ricky is more of an outdoorsman than I am, because he seemed to enjoy the tracking and trying to find out where the bulls went, and I just wanted to go home. I admit it—I was scared to death. Ricky later said he was scared but also curious and angry that they'd taken the bulls. Those bulls were starting to become good rodeo stars and worth some money.

We were able to track them for maybe two miles, then it got rocky and we lost all signs of anything. We were stymied, so we stopped to take a break, sitting under a tree and taking in the incredible landscape. We were on the side of a mountain and could see forever. Chet went with us, but he's not much of a tracker. He mostly sniffed around.

It was about then that I told Ricky I was starting to get a creepy feeling, like someone was watching us. He agreed that he felt it too, and we both got out our binoculars and started looking all around. It wasn't long before I noticed several distant figures in a meadow way down below us.

I motioned to Ricky to take a look, and he said it was the two bulls, who were trying to graze, along with some other cattle. I say trying to graze because they would eat, then look up and around like they were nervous.

"If that's our bulls, you know who has to be nearby," Ricky said. "So what do we do now? Try to herd them back home?"

"Isn't that why we're here?" I asked. "If we don't get them now, we'll probably never see them again." I sounded brave, but deep inside, all I really wanted to do was go home. I was actually willing to give up on the bulls and any associated income just to get out of there.

OK, I neglected to mention a critical detail here, mostly because we were breaking the law, and I hate to incriminate myself. But it is part of the story, so here goes.

Ricky and I are seasoned dirt-bike riders. We'd ridden our bikes all over everywhere ever since we were kids. We lived next to wilderness areas and knew not to ride there, but we rode everywhere else.

But we'd been pretty upset about these bulls and had made the decision to ride wherever we needed to go to track them down. We tried to be careful, and we knew there was a chance we could get busted for it, but it seemed the only way we could catch up with any kind of livestock, especially critters with huge feet. Chet's a good rider and always rode behind Ricky.

So, we headed down to that beautiful meadow lickety-split, even though it was a wilderness area and mechanized vehicles weren't allowed. We would use the bikes to round up the cattle and herd them back.

We made it down to where the bulls now stood, staring at us. We began pushing them and the rest of the cattle slowly towards home. The whole time, I can tell you I was looking out for some kind of

Bigfoot or large creature to come stomping through to try to stop us, but we didn't see anything.

The bulls were easy to handle, as if they understood where we were going. There were a good ten other cows and steers that followed along.

We hadn't gone very far when I heard that strange noise coming from back in the trees. It made us light a fire under everything and start trotting the cattle along, though they kind of did this on their own. I'll never forget how scared they all looked.

We were finally about a half-mile from the house when our good luck ran out. At that point, everything seemed kind of chaotic, the cattle just plowing ahead and us following. But the strange noise sounded very close, not far behind us, and all of a sudden both of our dirtbikes shut off.

I mean, they both stopped running, just like that. Nothing would turn over, no starter noise or anything, just dead in the dirt. And the cattle hadn't slowed down any and were soon about to disappear over a rise, Chet at their heels.

To say I felt like someone in a bad movie who is about to meet their fate would be an understatement.

"Run, Wyatt!" Ricky yelled over and over as he took off, not bothering to see if I was following or not. He was smart, because he didn't take the time to see what I saw, and he doesn't now have bad dreams about it like I do.

I spun around, knowing there was something behind me, but not guessing how close it was. I caught a glimpse of a glowing blue creature the size of one of the bulls, which is to say, really big. It was real and had substance, and yet seemed wispy and like I could almost push through it.

But it was not something I wanted to push through, as it had a face that reminded me of pictures I'd seen of gorillas deep in the forest, with deep-sunk eyes and lips pushed out and forehead kind of slanting back. But its eyes were intelligent looking, and it was tall and, like I said, glowed with a blue light. Even as I saw it and my mind tried to make sense of it, I was thinking there was no reason it should glow like that.

I could also tell it moved fast. Of course, by then I was myself trying to move fast, but Ricky and Chet and the cattle had all disappeared over that rise above us.

I ran and ran, expecting it to grab me by the neck and pull me off my feet, but instead, it moved on past me as if it was more interested in the cattle. And as it went past, I could feel an electrical charge go through me.

I took this as my chance to veer off into the trees out of sight. There was a small ravine that I knew came out near the house, and I climbed up it, finally coming out near the barn, where I could see Dad and Chet and Ricky standing by the corral, which was now full of bulls and cattle.

Dad must've seen them coming and opened the gate. He was throwing out hay. I walked over to see a look of relief come across Ricky's face.

Neither of us said a word, and Ricky went inside and soon returned with the pickup keys. We hooked up dad's stock trailer and had our two bulls loaded up just as the neighbor drove up. We knew Dad had called him, thinking the cattle had to be his, which they were.

We helped him load up his stock in his trailer, then we set out with our trailer for the stockyards in the nearest town, where we would leave the bulls and where they would sell them for us.

Once the bulls were unloaded and fed and watered, we decided to go eat at a nearby restaurant. Neither of us were in a hurry to go home, and even Chet, who waited in the pickup, seemed happy to be away from the place, but maybe I was just projecting how I felt.

Ricky knew something had happened, and he asked if I wanted to talk about it, to which I simply said no. Today is the first time he's heard any of the details of what I saw, and I probably won't ever talk about it again. It really messed with my sense of what's real. To this day, I have no idea why Bigfoot took our stock, except to have something to eat at some point.

So, we finally went home, where we talked our parents into selling the place. It was an easy decision, for they'd already been talking about moving closer to town. Mom immediately moved into Tumwater with her sister, and Ricky and I moved near there and started a carpet-cleaning business.

Dad stayed up at the home place for a few days packing things up, but then called us and said he was having a really rough time of it, hearing strange noises and again seeing that blue light. He came down and stayed with Mom, and we all went and packed during the daytime. He ended up selling the ranch to our neighbor, who let his hired hand live there. He mostly wanted it for the hayfields.

It was an interesting page out of our family history on the ranch, but even having seen what I did, I wasn't prepared for when we were cleaning out the house's attic. There were some old journal entries made by my great-grandmother. Most of them were about the weather and what was blooming and such, as she had a big garden.

She mentioned setting loaves of bread on the fence posts for the creatures. I figured this was just for the birds until I saw an entry saying she was all out of bread and hoped there would be no damage that night. This leads me to believe that she was also dealing with the same thing we saw, or maybe its predecessors. She was feeding them as a type of bribe to leave her family alone.

In any case, I'm glad we're no longer up there to deal with it.

———

4

DEADMAN'S COVE

My travels are pretty limited in scope, mostly consisting of trips into Montana to help out a good buddy when he needs an extra fishing guide. Most of my time is spent in northwestern Colorado, where, since the birth of our child, I've been more of a stay at home dad. It seems like the times I do travel is when my wife Sarah has a seminar or some kind of work and we decide to accompany her.

This particular story came from a trip to Ellensburg, Washington, where Sarah was invited to give a talk to a geology class. I decided it would be fun to go along, not knowing that part of the country all that well. Central Washington is really pretty, and Ellensburg has a beautiful campus there at Central Washington University.

They have a great geology department with a fairly new building, and they've made a nice walk showcasing some large Washington rocks. I was walking around with our daughter showing her the rocks when we came across a fellow sitting nearby with his beautiful husky. My daughter had to pet the dog, with permission of course, and that led to a pretty good conversation about dogs, then fishing, then the back country, and eventually, Logan told the following story.

—Rusty

. . .

R usty, this was a once in a lifetime thing for me, at least so I hope. I never want to see anything like it again, and some nights I wake up wondering if I really saw what I did, or if it was just an hallucination.

If my dog Jake hadn't reacted like he did, I think I would have to write it off as my mind playing tricks on me or some such thing, though it would be a pretty elaborate trick. But Jake saw it, too, and the way he reacted told me it was real.

Sometimes I think it upset him as much as it did me, for he wouldn't even eat for a few days afterwards, and to this day he doesn't want to go to the beach. I guess it's a good thing we live in Ellensburg in central Washington, not near the ocean, but now he doesn't even like going to lakes, which he used to love.

So, I guess I'm going to have to say that for all of you out there who want a Bigfoot encounter, be careful what you wish for. If it effects you like it did me and Jake, you'll wish it had never happened.

Having it be far off near the ocean helps some, but I am aware of all the stories from all over the state, so even going out around home seems sketchy anymore. Washington's probably not the best place to live if you're afraid of Bigfoot, and it seems like the state is Ground Zero for Bigfoot in a sense, with all the stories from here. I guess I'll add mine to the list.

This happened at Cape Disappointment in a rainy July. You probably know the area, as it's a state park that juts into the Pacific Ocean at the tip of the Long Beach Peninsula in the southwestern corner of Washington. It's where Lewis and Clark ended their journey to the sea.

It was named Cape Disappointment when a British trader was searching for where the Columbia River entered the ocean and thought this area was only a bay. The Columbia does actually enter the Pacific here through a narrow channel.

OK, it was July, kind of the peak of tourist season and a good time to stay home, but a friend asked me if I was going to go photograph the king tides at Disappointment. I'd talked about going every year for some time, so I guess she was reminding me it was time. You can also see them in January, but it's cold and stormy.

The reason that the king tides come these two times of year has something to do with how far the moon and sun are from the earth, but I don't remember the details. All I know is that Washington's king tides are higher than Hawaii's, but lower than Alaska's.

When the tide is over 8 feet, huge waves crash into the cliffs at Cape Disappointment, making for great photos. To add interest, a big storm was predicted to come through, and when you have king tides on top of ocean swells, things can get really exciting.

I downloaded tide tables from the Internet, made a three-night reservation at a hotel in the nearby town of Ilwaco, threw my overnight stuff and camera gear into the car, and Jake and I headed out. It was early Saturday morning, and we were going to finally see the king tides at Cape Disappointment. I had taken Monday off work, so I figured we had plenty of time. We'd spend Saturday and Sunday at the park, then head home Monday.

The closer I got, the more excited I became! I'd talked about this for years, and it wasn't all that far, not like going to Hawaii or something, yet I'd never followed through. But now it was time. I would finally get to take some good photos and enjoy the park. I couldn't believe I'd never been there. And since it was dog friendly, I could have Jake on a leash with me.

A few hours later I'd checked into the motel and was at the Lewis and Clark Visitor Center for the park. I was shocked at how crowded it was—people lined the pathways, and the parking lot was full. Everyone was here to see the king tides. I finally found a spot to park. I got my camera gear and my daypack with some snacks and water ready to go.

We were quickly in an old-growth forest on the Cape Disappointment Trail, going to the Cape Disappointment Lighthouse. We'd only gone a short distance when I saw a trail that looked like it was going down to the shore.

Jake is really gentle with strangers, but people were everywhere and it was hard to take him on the trail without bumping into people who were half-afraid of dogs, so I decided to see where this side trail went.

People were on this trail, too, but it wasn't crowded, probably because it was steep and muddy. Someone had built stairs going down the treacherous slope, but the bottom few were washed out.

As I descended, I could see I was going into a tight little cove with tall cliffwalls and a short beach with lots of driftwood. Several people were playing fetch with their dogs, and Jake thought this would be a swell thing to do, so when I got down there I threw a stick for him, though he was pretty distracted by the other dogs.

This was one of the most picturesque places I'd ever been, and I was soon enjoying taking lots of photos, especially of the small island where the ocean entered the cove between tall cliffs. A lone pine tree grew from the top of the island, which was more like a big rock.

I noticed someone had swam out there and was standing on the tallest part of the rock, which I found somewhat irritating, as it was messing with my nature photos.

Later, I was looking at my photos on the computer and tried to zoom in on that figure up on the rocks, and what I saw wasn't conclusive, but its size scaled against that tree and the rocks sure made me think it wasn't human after all.

I found out later that this little cove was called Deadman's Cove. I love beautiful places with sad names, but I'm not so fond of the place as I was when we first saw it. I'll explain in a minute.

The reason it was called Deadman's Cove was because apparently bodies would end up here from the many shipwrecks that were common in the day. The area is called the Graveyard of the Pacific because of all the shipwrecks. The force of the Columbia flowing into the ocean here creates one of the most treacherous bars in the world, and over 234 ships have sank near the mouth of the river.

OK, I guess I forgot something really important that I should mention at this point. When I got down to the beach, I was feeling a bit dizzy. I sat down on a big log for a while and watched people playing with their dogs, then I was OK.

I took lots of good photos and had fun playing with Jake, but when I saw the figure on the rock, I started feeling dizzy again.

Now don't get me wrong, I'm not attributing my dizziness to the figure on the rock, and at that point in time I really did think it was a person. I know people have had strange experiences accompany Bigfoot sightings, but I actually have high-blood pressure, and sometimes the medication I take for it will make me feel a little dizzy, so I basically attributed the way I felt to my health. But since I'm not 100 percent sure about that, I'll just throw that fact into the mix with everything else to consider.

I had been on the beach probably a half hour when the king waves started in full force. Some big waves had been breaking across the small cove when I got there, but the fact that the cove was so sheltered had kept them smaller.

But now the waves were getting bigger, and I became worried about what's called a sleeper wave, though I wasn't sure the topography in the cove was good enough to create one. A sleeper wave can appear out of nowhere, especially during storms. They're much bigger than normal waves and sneak up on you because they're infrequent and unexpected.

You might see a half hour or more of regular waves, then all of the sudden a wave twice the size of the others rolls all the way up the beach carrying driftwood logs. Such waves can be very dangerous.

I decided it was probably time to get out of there and go on up to the lighthouse, which I had heard was a pretty stiff hike, though not far. I wanted to take photos of the views from up there, because I heard you can see the mouth of the Columbia, as well as far out to the ocean. Plus, the lighthouse itself is pretty cool.

I started back up the steep stairs when I heard the most chilling sound I've ever heard in my life. It was high-pitched and really loud, kind of like a jet engine would sound as it starts warming up, really high and shrill. It sounded like it was coming from the cove below, and as I stood there in shock, I wondered if the person on the island had left or not.

For a minute, I thought it was that person, as it seemed to be coming from that direction, but I saw no one there. The scream seemed to last about five to ten seconds, and though it was mostly high-pitched, it also had a vibrato to it.

I could now see huge waves breaking across the mouth of the cove, and I continued climbing the stairs. Everyone else came rushing up the trail, and I'd say that scream had the same effect on us all—we were terrified. I kept tripping over Jake as he tried to outrun me back to the car.

Once at the very top, I turned and looked back again, and this time I could see a huge wave hammering the beach. I guess the king waves did affect the cove, and I was glad I'd left. I got a few photos, in spite of being pretty flustered by the scream, but at that point I had made sense of it by deciding it was a mountain lion.

Back at the main trail, I almost went back to my car. I was starting to feel kind of shaken up, but my desire to take more photos won out. Everything was so lush and green, and the huge waves were spellbinding with the sea mist rolling through the trees like a wispy fog. Jake wanted to go back, but I'd decided to go on to the lighthouse. There were plenty of people on the trail, so I felt pretty safe.

It was a stiff mile, but not that bad, and once up there, I got in a few photos before the clouds and mist moved in and it started raining. There would be no more photography.

I decided to go back to the interpretive center for awhile and watch the movie they had about the Lewis and Clark Expedition, then I would head back to the motel and get a hot dinner at a nearby café. Jake and I could always walk around town if the rain let up.

Well, on the way back, I made the mistake of stopping at the top of the trail down to Deadman's Cove, hoping I might get some good photos through the fog. Sometimes what they call atmospheric photos are the best.

I got to where I could see the beach below, and I could now see someone on the beach, motionless as if they were dead. Had someone been hit by a wave or maybe a piece of driftwood?

I felt like I should go see, as it's part of my nature to want to be helpful, but I knew the steps would be slick from the rain, plus I remembered that horrible scream, and had no desire to go back down there. I decided it would be best to find a ranger.

I got back to the interpretive center just as it closed. No rangers anywhere. I was ready to call it a day and go back to the motel, but the thought of someone injured on the beach stuck with me. I couldn't just leave and not do anything, could I? Surely someone else had also seen them, given the number of people on the trail. But then, it had been raining hard, and most everyone had left.

The last thing I wanted to do was go back, but my conscience wouldn't let me leave, so back down the trail I headed. Once I got to the top of the stairs, it stopped raining. I could clearly see the beach, and there was no one there. Either the person had recovered or someone else had rescued them.

I felt relieved. I could now go back and get some dinner and relax, then go through the photos I'd taken to see if I got any good ones.

But just then, the sun broke through, and one of the most beautiful rainbows I've ever seen appeared. It would've been really cool had it been framing the island with the tree, but I was at the wrong angle from the sun, and instead it fell on the rocks more to my left.

It had the most intense colors I've ever seen, and I suddenly felt like it would fulfill the dream of taking the most fantastic rainbow photo if I could just capture it. But that would require going down, at least partway, to the beach. Rainbows usually don't last very long, and I knew I had very little time to make it happen if I wanted a photo.

I hesitated, thinking once again of the scream, but my excitement overtook my common sense. I decided it had just been a mountain lion over in the trees, and the odds of it still being around were slim, and the odds of it bothering me were even slimmer, especially with Jake there.

I'd made my decision. I was quickly slipping and sliding down the trail, grabbing onto branches and whatever else I could find as I made my way down. It's a miracle I didn't fall and injure myself, but before I knew it, I was down on the beach.

I quickly got my camera out and ready, just in time to notice Jake wasn't with me. He was still standing at the top of the stairs! This is the dog that won't leave my side even when there are deer or rabbits to chase.

I was beyond puzzled. I called to him and he finally came down, though reluctantly, and I could see he was shaking like a leaf. He stayed as close to me as possible, pushing against my leg and whining.

OK, I'm not so dense that I will ignore these kind of warning signs from my normally quiet and easy-going dog. The rainbow was still hanging there in all its glory, so I took a few photos, put my camera back in its case, and headed for the stairs.

Jake was now ahead of me, wanting to leave as fast as possible and yet wanting to make sure I was coming along behind. This made him somewhat of a hazard, as he would go forward and then stop, making it so I would almost step on him. I would stop for a moment, then as he got going again I would go, then he would stop—well, you can see the pattern we were in trying to climb the stairs which made it rather slow.

We were almost to the top when I slipped and fell. I remember wondering whether anyone would ever find me or not. Fortunately, I didn't go very far before a small bush stopped me. Jake was soon by my side, and I managed to grab him by the tail, and he pulled me up to where I could get a foothold. I was covered in mud.

I was now basically crawling up the side of the hill, hanging on to Jake, trying not to slide backwards. I was almost back to the top when he stopped moving and started growling a deep sound that I'd never heard from him before.

He quickly jumped at something in the bushes, but was soon back by my side. I managed to find a flat spot and managed to stand up. Jake stood right next to me, his hackles up, still growling.

It was then that someone threw a large branch, nearly hitting me. It had been thrown with a good deal of force, for it whizzed by, and I remember thinking it would've really hurt if it had been on target. I was puzzled. Why would someone want to hit me with a big stick?

The branch had come from the direction of the beach, and as I looked down, I saw what I took to be that same black figure I'd seen on the island earlier, except now it was upright, looking directly at me, and I knew it had thrown the stick. I also knew it had to be very powerful to throw a stick that far.

My instincts were to run, but there was no way I could do that in the mud on that steep slope. So, I grabbed onto Jake again and said, "Let's go back." That was a phrase he knew well, as I said it when we were hiking and I was ready to turn around. He took off, pulling as hard as he could.

I still shake my head with disbelief when I think about how quickly that creature climbed that steep slope, especially in the mud. I hadn't gone more than a good 20 feet when Jake stopped and turned around, growling. I turned just in time to see this creature right behind me.

I was too shocked to really process what I was seeing, but I will say it was huge and lanky. It looked like a tall basketball player with long black-brown hair except for around its face, where it was just black skin. I read a lot of accounts where they say it was muscular like a football player, but this one was just tall and thin, though not terribly so.

And those eyes—they were dark yellow and looked like they could see right through you. And the look on its face was pure malice. I can only describe it as being a toxic-looking mixture of anger and bad intent.

Jake was now trying to hide behind me, and in doing so, knocked me back down. Later, when I saw myself in the motel mirror, I realized I looked like I'd been in some kind of mud-wrestling contest. I also realized how dizzy I'd suddenly become as the creature was heading toward us, just like I'd been when down on the beach earlier.

As I fell, Jake came down on top of me. The timing was such that this creature thing flew over us, though in retrospect, I'm not sure it was going after us at all, in spite of the branch it lobbed at us.

I ducked down, certain it was going to attack me, even though I could barely think at all, I was in such a state of disbelief. I at first decided it was someone in a suit, but I knew deep inside no one could scale that steep trail that fast, especially in the mud. And the ruts it left behind said it had to weigh a lot—seriously, it actually left ruts in the trail where it had climbed out.

It was all over in a moment, and the creature was gone, headed back to the main trail. It has started raining again, so I doubt if there was anyone there to see it.

I have no idea what was going on. Maybe it was angry that I was in its territory, or maybe there was something else going on out past me and on back at the main trail. I'll never know, which is OK by me.

I managed to get back up, but it was hard to stand, as I was still dizzy. After awhile, I was starting to get back to normal, and Jake and I made it back to the main trail. Since that trail is paved, we made good time getting back to the interpretive center and my car. I was paranoid the whole way back, thinking we were going to see this thing again, but we didn't.

We went back to the motel, got cleaned up, I packed my bags, and we headed home. It was late when we got in, but I didn't care. I just wanted to be away from that place.

It took me some time to get over it, though I'm not sure I really have completely. Jake developed a fear of going near water and into the woods, and when I would try to take him hiking with me he wouldn't even get out of the car. To be honest, I wasn't that keen on hiking in the woods anymore either.

We ended up finding several good places around town that we could get exercise, like the parks, and we would even go down and walk around the college campus some, which is beautiful.

This should be the end of the story, but there's more. It wasn't long after that when I saw a post on social media about how the Cape Disappointment Lighthouse had been having strange things happen.

As far as I know, the lighthouse is managed by the Coast Guard. You can visit it but not go inside. Anyway, a number of people have said they've seen someone recklessly climbing the building like a monkey would, just scaling it without ropes or anything, and really quickly.

I don't know how this would be possible, but supposedly someone has photos of it. But just like my photo of the stranger standing on the rock island in Deadman's Cove, they're probably inconclusive and hard to define.

It seems that Bigfoot photos are like that in general. I think it's because people are so shaken up they don't even think about photos. I know if I had been able to take a photo of the creature as it passed by me, I would probably either be famous or told I was a hoaxer.

But it doesn't matter, because seeing that face again in real life is the last thing I would ever want, as I see it often enough in my nightmares.

———

5

THE BOGGY MARSH MONSTER

Not all of the Bigfoot stories I collect come from my fishing clients, and, as I mentioned before, some come from my wife Sarah's geology contacts. This makes sense, as geologists typically spend a lot of time outdoors doing field work, though not all do.

Sammy was one of Sarah's college friends who stopped by one evening for dinner while in the area. His story makes me wonder a lot about how Bigfoot deal with their dead.

—Rusty

At the time this happened, I was a graduate student at a university, doing field work studying the Cascadia Subduction Zone, the 700-mile fault that runs from northern California up to British Columbia.

A lot of people don't know that the Pacific Northwest is a major earthquake zone. The Cascadia fault has had 43 earthquakes in the last 10,000 years, and the last one was on January 26, 1700, with an estimated 9.0 magnitude.

That's a huge earthquake, and it caused the coastline to actually drop several feet. A tsunami inundated the coast, burying the regional salt marshes in sand.

How do you study the effects of something that happened that long ago? How do we know with such accuracy when the earthquake happened? It took some sleuthing, and part of the evidence came from Japanese historical records, which indicated that a destructive tsunami struck their coast on January 26, 1700, yet there weren't any nearby earthquakes.

By studying the flow of the Pacific Ocean, we can link the tsunami in Japan with this great Cascadia earthquake, and we also have evidence from Native American legends.

And there's much more evidence, which was what I was studying —deposits of sand in estuaries near the coast, which showed a huge tsunami had hit the area around that time. There's also evidence from tree rings. By dating the time the sand was deposited and the trees stopped growing, it all fits together, and we can date the earthquake.

So, I was studying tidal wetland stratigraphic sequences, which is just another way of saying that I was looking at the layers of soil and plant matter in cores that I took from different spots in marshes and along tidal waterways. All the cores showed sand deposits around the time of the big quake, more evidence of a huge tsunami. There were also other layers showing previous tsunamis.

A lot of studies have been done on the big Cascadia quake, and my goal was to provide further verification of all this through more samples, to see how far the tsunami had gone inland. I worked from a canoe, paddling around, climbing onto the banks of these tidal waterways and marshes, taking core samples. Part of my work attire was hip waders, and I was always soggy, muddy, and wet.

A lot of science consists of collecting data. You have to have the information before you can determine what actually happened. My cores were interesting, most showing a layer of sand that meant the tsunami had come quite a distance inland. They showed that layers rich with vegetation were buried in sand, the plants then dying.

Forests and thickly vegetated marshes had been replaced by barren tidal flats.

So, I spent a lot of time collecting data in the field, and I got a lot of good samples, but I also found something I didn't expect to find, something I really wished I *hadn't* found—something science has yet to explain, though I probably came as close to finding the necessary evidence as anyone has yet. But it slipped away, and no one knows where it went.

That sounds really strange, but it's exactly what happened, though I often wonder if it didn't float away. Let me explain.

I don't recall the exact day, but I do remember I was tired and thinking of taking a week or two off. It was mid-summer, and my life had consisted of nothing but wading in the muck and bogs, grinding out core samples, loading them into the canoe, then taking them to what I'd set up as a makeshift lab in a room of one of the old buildings on campus. I would analyze them later when the weather turned and I wasn't able to get out in the field.

I would then write my thesis on what I'd found, defend it in front of my committee, then have a master's degree in geology. What I would do then was anybody's guess, as I hadn't really thought about it. Hopefully get a good job with some state entity, as geology jobs were hard to come by.

So, I was out puttering around in my canoe, trying not to scare the wildlife, going from shore to shore in a marsh near Puget Sound, thinking about what I would do if I did take a week or two off.

I had just taken a good sample when I thought I saw a blue heron land nearby. Wetlands usually teem with life, from herons to dragonflies, and I had actually started keeping a journal of the plants and wildlife I saw in each salt marsh.

It included lily pads, a family of river otters playing at the edge of the lily pads, six turtles on a log, deer, a cottonwood tree with fresh beaver gnawings, garter snakes (there are no poisonous snakes native to the Seattle area), a beaver lodge, water-striders, a short-tailed weasel, willows and cattails, and all kinds of birds, including a nest full of baby purple martins. There's more, but you get the idea.

So, I wanted to see if this was indeed a blue heron, and I could then add it to my list. I don't know why, but I like making lists—maybe it makes me feel organized, which I'm not. But I later added one simple entry to that list—one I had never dreamed I would add, a rather ominous entry.

Anyway, I pulled up to shore, got out of my canoe, climbed the bank, and started in the direction I'd seen the heron go. I was immediately in tall grasses, a big marshy area next to a forest of huge red cedars.

The only other person I've ever told this to is my friend Erin, and she just shakes her head. I know she doesn't believe me, but she did ask if I had a premonition that something strange was going on. The funny thing was, I didn't. Nothing felt different or strange or anything, well, at least not at first. It was just another marsh like all the others I'd collected samples from.

I took out my little pocket binoculars to check around for the heron. This was a nice diversion from drilling more core samples, which was hard work. I started walking around, looking through the binoculars every so often, kind of working my way to the edge of the cedar trees.

It was about then that I spotted something different. It looked like a small mound out in the grasses. I headed toward it, and as I did, a sudden feeling of dread swept over me like a rogue wave from nowhere. I think it was my subconscious telling me I was about to encounter something weird and that maybe I should just turn around and go back. I wish I had.

But I didn't. I kept going, and the closer I got to the small mound the odder it looked, and by that, I mean it didn't look natural. It was just shaped different, is all I can say, and I could now see that it was a uniform dark green color.

OK, it had to be some kind of stand of unusual plants, in fact, it kind of looked like ferns, the kind you'd see in the deep forest, not in a marsh. I decided it was some kind of forest plant that had managed to grow in the marsh.

The closer I got, the more ominous it felt, until I was pretty sure I should just get the heck out of there and go home. I needed a vacation, I decided. The hard work was getting to me.

But my curiosity was greater than my fear, because I kept going. I was soon standing over something my mind couldn't decipher—it was some kind of huge body wrapped in ferns, like some kind of death shroud.

I stood dumbfounded for what seemed like forever, but I know it was only a minute or two, trying to figure out what I was looking at.

First, it was huge, like a Sumo wrestler, though much taller, and it looked like it could weigh as much as a small horse. I couldn't make out anything except size, as it was completely wrapped in ferns, with mud plastered on them to hold them onto the body. It looked like it had been there for some time, as the mud had cracked.

I could see a few tufts of long brown hair where the mud had crinkled up, and that was all I needed. I carried a small camera around my neck, but the thought of taking photos of it seemed disrespectful, plus I didn't want anything to remind me of what I was looking at. I felt like I was in some kind of horror movie, and at that point, all I wanted to do was flee, which I did.

I remember running through the marsh, splashing water all over, thinking that I had to be really careful to not fall or it could be the end of my life. I don't know why, as nothing had threatened me. It was just a feeling of general doom.

Once back at my canoe, it occurred to me that I should've taken a GPS reading, even though I had no intention of going back. I did take one there where I'd stopped, which would be helpful if I ever did decide to return—or maybe as a marker telling me to not stop there.

I was soon back at my pickup, loading the canoe, soon on my way home. I'll never forget walking in the front door and feeling an immediate sense of safety and security, the opposite of what I'd felt out in the marsh.

Well, I decided to take a vacation. I would drive down to Portland and visit my friend Erin, taking my time, camping in state parks on the way. I would visit the Copalis Ghost Forest, which is near Gray's Harbor.

This forest of red cedars is for the most part still standing like it was before the trees died, though now they look like ghostly gray poles. It's in a muddy tidal flat, having dropped over six feet from the earthquake. It was then completely inundated with salt water, turning the dense forest into a marsh.

There are a number of ghost forests along the coast all the way from Washington into Mendocino, California, as that's where the Cascadia fault ends.

Tree rings from these forests show they all died at the same time, and by comparing their rings to trees still alive, scientists were able to determine the trees had stopped growing after completing the 1699 growing season, which would have been sometime between September of 1699 and May of 1700.

The ghost forest can be reached only by boat from the middle of the town of Copalis Beach, so I loaded up my canoe. Once there, it would be a two-mile round-trip paddle, and I planned on staying at a nearby state park.

I drove straight there, as it wasn't all that far, and I noted that I still felt kind of odd from the previous day's find, whatever it was. I could still see in my mind's eye the large body lying there, wrapped in ferns, and I was now wondering if I shouldn't have notified the local authorities. What if it was someone who'd been murdered?

I needed to go back if I was going to tell anyone about it, for they would need the GPS coordinates. The marsh was just too big to say there's a body in the marsh. They would never find it.

This bothered me all the way down the coast to Copalis Beach. I almost decided to skip the ghost forest and drive on down to Portland, not even camping, but just go straight to Erin's house.

I did make one stop, which was to get a cup of coffee and a muffin in a little drive-through espresso place. I sat in my truck for awhile, trying to figure out why my normal state of mind was gone, though I knew why. It was from finding the body, and I wished I had never gone looking for that blue heron. I was beginning to feel haunted.

I was soon in the small town of Copalis Beach, where I unloaded my canoe and headed for the ghost forest, even though my heart wasn't in it. I was soon there, an eerie landscape of logs sticking out of muddy tidal flats.

It was the last place I needed to be. I felt like I was on another planet, and what I needed was to be in a place that felt grounded and homey, not alien. The ghost forest made me feel even more haunted than before.

I didn't stay long, especially when I heard a weird howling noise in the distance. I decided later that it was just a coyote, but it really set me on edge.

I was soon back at my truck, and instead of heading on down to Portland, I decided to go home. I somehow had to deal with my mental state. Erin wouldn't understand. She was a fellow scientist and was very pragmatic, the same as I normally was, until I'd seen the strange body, that is. My scientific paradigm couldn't explain it, and I wouldn't be able to rest mentally until I figured it out.

I knew this meant I had to go back to the marsh. I'd go out the next day.

Back home, I made some dinner and tried to get lost in a movie, but I was too distracted and kept losing track of what was going on, so I finally turned it off.

I didn't sleep well at all and was up earlier than usual, anxious to just get it over with. I would go visit the site of the body, get a GPS reading, hightail it out of there, then report it and head on back toward Portland. Maybe that would ease the mental turmoil I was in.

It seemed to take forever to get out there, but I was eventually back out at the location my GPS said I'd beached the boat and started out. I hesitated to leave my boat, but I finally climbed the bank and tried to follow my earlier path.

Nothing looked the same—or I should say, everything looked the same. It looked like every other marsh I'd been in, and scoping things with my binoculars didn't help any.

Finally, I recognized a beautiful stand of Douglas aster. I'd stopped by it before to admire the purple flowers. I then knew that the body wasn't far, just across the marsh a few hundred feet.

Knowing I was near it made me queasy, and I vowed to get there as fast as I could, take a GPS reading, then high-tail it back to my canoe.

It was then that I noticed the marsh grasses were flattened along a path, not as if something had been dragged along, but rather as if huge footsteps had made it. It headed toward where I thought the body was.

I followed the path to where I knew the body must be, but all that was there was a flattened place where the grasses were smashed down. The body was gone, and all that was left were a few shreds of ferns, enough to make me certain I'd found the right spot.

I shivered, took a GPS reading anyway, though I had no idea why, then turned and hurried back to my canoe as fast as I could, suddenly feeling that sense of doom I'd felt before.

Back at my boat, I slipped in, relieved. But as I pushed away from shore, I saw something that made the hairs on my neck stand up— huge tracks in the mud—a *lot* of them—and next to them, more smashed ferns. As I pushed off, now in a panic, I could see ferns floating in the water near my canoe.

It was now looking like the body had been carried down to the shore, then dumped in the water. *Carried* down, not dragged, and whatever carried it had to be big and strong, because that body was huge. Like I said, it looked like it weighed as much as a small horse.

I shivered, then started rowing as hard as I could. For all I could tell, it looked like the body had been carried by *several* somethings just as big. I half-expected to see the body floating on the water.

I knew they were still around, and I nearly fell into the water when I heard an intense howl coming from not far behind me, and I knew it wasn't a coyote.

And then, to make things worse, it was answered by another howl ahead of me, somewhere along the estuary I was paddling through. It would be awhile before I could get out in the open, and those moments felt like years, but I finally made it and was back at my pickup.

I loaded the canoe, then got in and locked the doors, forcing myself to take some deep breaths so I wouldn't panic. I couldn't afford to wreck my truck by driving too fast, given the mental state I was in.

Finally home, I realized there would be no need to call the authorities, as it wasn't a human body. I didn't want to admit what I thought it was, but I knew it was a Sasquatch, or Bigfoot.

I pulled up Google Earth, put in the GPS coordinates, and studied the landscape. A well-worn path led from the coordinates straight into the nearby forest, where I could no longer follow it because of the trees. Searching all around, I then found another trail that led from the forest into nearby hills, where it again disappeared as if going into a cave.

It was puzzling, but impossible to determine anything from. Maybe a more courageous explorer would've gone back and hiked it, but not me. I hadn't seen it when out there because I was too busy trying to get far away.

It certainly put a different light on my research, wandering around those estuaries and marshes alone, and I finally decided I would write my thesis based on the cores I already had. I had quite a few, and if my advisor complained that I hadn't found enough evidence, well, I would just have to tell him why.

I then went to Erin's, foregoing the camping, as I knew I wasn't in a good enough mental state to be outdoors, especially at night. I ended up staying at her house for a few weeks, as she was going to visit her family and needed a dog sitter. It worked out great, as I got a lot of my thesis written.

I graduated and got a good job with a state entity, just as I'd planned, but not doing field work. I worked in an office, which was OK by me. And that office was in eastern Washington, far from marsh bogs.

Now, when I think of the Boggy Creek Monster movie, I think of what I found, though mine was more like a Boggy Marsh Monster. And as for Bigfoot, I'll add that sometimes you don't need to actually see it to know it's there.

———

6

THE GLIDERS

Bob had signed up for one of my all-day flyfishing seminars, and he enjoyed it so much he decided to go for a three-day trip. We were fishing the Yampa River, near my home in Colorado, and he seemed to be especially observant of the outdoors, taking the time to examine things and ask questions about the flora and fauna, which most fisherpeople don't do, as they're focused on fishing. He also took a lot of photos.

Later, he told me he'd really been missing the outdoors, and since I didn't want to pry, I just said I could never live without being able to get out, but I did wonder why he hadn't been outside much. It wasn't until the last day of fishing, after our Dutch-oven dinner, that he and I got to talking. He told me why he hadn't felt comfortable outside, though he said he was getting over it, and he and his wife were hoping to get out more.

—Rusty

My wife and I live in Portland, but we used to go quite often to Forlorn Lakes, which are in Washington, but only a two-hour drive from our house. The lakes are in Skamania County, which is pretty famous for Bigfoot stories, though we only found this out later.

We had no interest in the subject until this happened, and we've now done a lot of research and read many stories from there. In case you're not familiar with the region, it's the home of Mount St. Helens and Mount Adams right on its border, and also the Columbia River Gorge. The Pacific Crest Trail passes through the area, and almost 90 percent of the county is timberland, mostly within the Gifford Pinchot National Forest.

Some of the stories from Skamania County will make your hair stand on end, and there seem to be a lot of sightings. We later found out that our favorite camping area, Forlorn Lakes, was also a favorite of Bigfoot, based on the number of encounters people have had there, everything from hearing wood knocks to actually seeing the creatures.

Forlorn Lakes Campground is very popular, and the camping spots fill early in the week. The campground is unique in that the sites are not bunched together but are spread out along the shores of a chain of small lakes, making the sites generally very private, and just about every site has a lake view.

The lakes aren't very deep, but they're OK for light boating, with mostly small rowboats, paddleboards, and an occasional canoe. Motorized boats aren't allowed, which means the area is very serene.

There's a nearby cave called Guler Ice Cave that's fun to hike to. It's an exposed lava tube that's filled with ice formations for most of the year. A short walk from the parking area leads to a single flight of stairs down to the cave floor, and huckleberry bushes grow in the campground and surrounding area. My theory is that the huckleberries attract Bigfoot.

My wife, Terry, and I had camped at Forlorn Lakes for years and never had anything unusual happen, so we weren't prepared when all this usual activity came our way. But who would be? I mean, you'e out in the thick forest and even though there are people around, you're pretty much on your own, away from civilization with wildlands just out your door.

We owned a small paving business, mostly doing things like driveways and parking lots, and when we were busy, we couldn't just take a break like you can with some jobs, we always had to finish up first. So when we were between jobs, we would try to set aside a week or so once in awhile to take breaks.

This particular case was one of those breaks, and we set off to the lakes with a week's supply of food and water, as there's no drinking water at the lakes.

Part of the fun is being carefree and eating the stuff you don't eat at home, like barbecued meats and doughnuts (not at the same time, obviously). We do a lot of canoeing, so we figure we make up for the calories, and we just pretend our cholesterol is fine.

We also stay up late playing card games, usually poker. We'll build a fire and play until it dies out, then we go to bed in our 4-person tent, which we outfit with cots and chairs and rugs. Our dog, Barksey, has his own bed on the floor under one of the cots where he guards everything. We named him Barksey after the painter Banksey because he was always decorating things, if you know what I mean.

OK, it was getting late in the season, and we knew our time for being able to camp was coming to an end with winter. If I recall correctly, it was early October. We had a little tent heater that ran on propane, so we figured we would be OK if the nights were cold, as long as the days weren't too bad. We were eager to get out, as it had been over a month since we've been able to go anywhere.

We arrived in the early evening, the days now being shorter, and we had everything set up by dark. We'd decided to bring the canoe, knowing it would be our last chance to use it for the season. We both love the peaceful feeling you get just cruising quietly along the shore, and we knew we would probably be the only people there that late in the year.

By the time we got everything set up, fog began rolling in, making the forest look mysterious in the evening shadows. The canoe was still in its unlocked carrier on top of the car, and I wanted to go ahead and unload it, but Terry said we should leave it up there in case we got rained out. The weather forecast had been a bit iffy, calling for possible rains, but we'd decided to chance it anyway.

We're not experienced canoeists in the sense that we did it a lot, we just basically liked to float around lakeshores. Our canoe was an older model, one we'd picked up at a yard sale. It was pretty beat up, and we'd discussed buying a new one at the next sale we saw. So leaving it in the carrier wasn't a big deal, especially since we didn't figure anyone would want it enough to actually steal it, and there wasn't anyone around anyway.

Now, Rusty, having read a gazillion Bigfoot accounts since this happened, I've noticed there seems to be a pattern for encounters. Basically, you get camp set up, go to bed, then have unknown sounds and creatures terrify you in the middle of the night, along with howls and bad smells.

You then hide in your locked vehicle and leave the next day, though some people leave during the night. Rocks and limbs are often thrown into your camp, often before you go to bed, kind of setting you up to be terrified.

I'm not saying this isn't what happens to most people who see Bigfoot, but we had a different sort of experience. Maybe it was because we had Barksey with us. He's a Dachshund, a pretty small dog, and even though he had his own bed, he would usually end up under the covers with me or my wife by about 2 a.m. I think he sleeps cold, even though he has his own down sleeping bag.

That particular night, he chose me to sleep with, probably because we'd put his bed under my cot and I was closest. I'm not sure what time it was, but I woke to him growling, then I saw a shadow through our nylon tent, there being an almost full moon. My first thought was a bear was outside, but when I opened one of the tent windows a bit I could see what looked like a large moose.

It dumped the pan with our silver and dishes off the picnic table, making a huge noise which made it run back into the bushes. Barksey settled down and we all went back to sleep.

No strange noises or Bigfoot calls or the sound of owls talking to each other (another Bigfoot clue), just a beautiful sunrise with rays cutting through low-lying fog, hitting nearby trees and lighting up their tops. I managed to get up in time to get some great photos.

I'll add here that at the time, I didn't know that the few thousand moose in Washington are in the remote mountains of the north-eastern part of the state, with small numbers in the North Cascades. They've supposedly been seen in southern Washington, though are rare.

Thinking back on it later, I know I was trying to fit something into a shape that made sense, but I'm not sure that was actually what I saw.

Terry made some delicious pancakes for breakfast, and Barksey buried the bites she gave him under the table (which I now think may have help attracted the "wildlife" that came into camp that night). Since it was now looking like it would clear off, we decided to take the canoe out, float around, and explore.

We had a peaceful day floating around the lake, just what we needed after a busy work week. The lake had several small arms that we explored that were especially marshy. Barksey even had fun. Dachshunds aren't known for being water dogs, but he really likes canoeing, as long as he doesn't get wet. We have a small life jacket he wears.

It was getting on toward late afternoon when the fog started rolling back in. We were out in the farthest section of the lake from camp when we decided we'd better head back. It suddenly hit me that I was really tired, and it became all I could do to paddle.

I asked Terry how she felt, and she gave me an odd look and said she was exhausted. This didn't make sense, as we'd barely been moving all day, just floating around. Even Barksey looked tired and wanted onto Terry's lap, even though she was rowing.

It was then that I thought I saw something back in the bushes that didn't blend in, something black. Thinking it was another moose, and knowing they can be grumpy and dangerous, I told Terry we needed to get back to camp.

She pointed back toward the way we'd come, and I could now see where two heads seemed to float through the marshy part of the lake, their bodies hidden by fog.

Their posture made it look like they were sitting in a boat, gliding behind a small wall of reeds. What was odd was that they made no movement, kind of like a cardboard cutout, and they were really large and looked like they had beards or lots of hair or both. They soon disappeared into the shadows, never turning their heads our way.

We both agreed it felt really creepy, and we upped our pace back to camp. Once there, we pulled the canoe onto shore, then made some dinner and quickly went into the tent as the fog moved back in, now totally engulfing everything.

We talked about going home early, though neither of us wanted to. But things felt different, kind of off, and it was beginning to make us both uncomfortable, yet there was no explanation why. The only thing we'd seen that was odd was the floating heads, and we knew they had to be someone in a boat, probably camped on up the lake.

We didn't feel like doing much, so we talked a little, keeping our voices low, feeling as if someone might be listening in, though we had no reason to think this.

Finally, Terry proposed we go home, as we weren't enjoying ourselves, even though it was now pitch dark, the full moon an obscured orb high above the thick clouds.

I agreed we should go home, but by the time we'd talked it through, we both felt too tired to pack up, especially since it was starting to drizzle. So much for the nice weather that had been forecast. We now worried we'd get caught in a snowstorm, but we were too tired to do anything about it.

Next thing I knew, Barksey was scratching at my sleeping bag, trying to get down inside. He seemed frantic, and after I pulled him down inside with me, I could feel him breathing really hard, like he was scared. He started whimpering, and if you know Dachshunds, they aren't whimperers, but are instead some of the bravest dogs on the planet. I'd never seen him this way.

Terry was still sleeping, so I slipped out of my bag and into my boots, pulling my coat on over my longjohns. The little propane heater had run out of fuel, so I grabbed another bottle and was hooking it up when I could hear something breathing, something outside and right next to the tent.

I froze. Whatever it was, it was standing only a few feet from me, just on the other side of the tent wall. Nylon isn't much of a barrier, and I suddenly felt really vulnerable. I knew Barksey was afraid of something, but what was it? A bear? It was October, and I figured the bears were already starting to hibernate.

It felt different from a bear, which I know makes no sense, but my intuition said it was something I needed to get far away from. I couldn't leave Terry and Barksey in the tent, plus I had nowhere to go, as the car wasn't close enough to outrun something big.

I went from being terrified to being calm in a brief second, for I decided whatever it was, I had no way to control what it did. This realization was a form of acceptance.

When you're out in the wilds, you have to accept that you're no longer at the top of the food chain if you want to enjoy yourself, otherwise, you're always on edge. But later, I felt like something had made me relax, maybe some kind of mind control, though that sounds totally insane.

I went back to fixing the propane, which basically just meant screwing a one-pound bottle onto the small heater, then turning it on and lighting it. A little propane always leaks out when you first turn it on, and lighting it always has a whoosh sound with a little flame burst.

When this happened, I could hear whatever it was outside run away, making some noise through the grasses, even though they were wet. I then heard a crack sound, and then something hit the tent.

I finally got up the courage to slip outside to see what had happened, and I found a large branch lying against the tent. Something had broken it off and thrown it at us. This is, of course, standard Bigfoot stuff, though I didn't know it at the time.

I shone my big flashlight all around, but saw nothing—but wait! There was something in the shadows at the tree line. My light revealed for a brief moment a head that looked like a cardboard cutout, just like what we'd seen out on the lake, but it ducked and quickly disappeared.

I went back to bed, angry and irritated. Terry never did wake up, and Barksey eventually settled down.

OK, our new neighbors were somehow trying to rob our camp. It's funny how your mind tries to fill in the gaps when you can't make sense of something. I decided it was someone trying to steal stuff, and my decision was verified when the next morning we found our canoe missing.

I was now even more irritated. I was ready to get in our car and drive around to various campsites to see who had the canoe when Terry, who'd been walking Barksey along the lake, came back to camp and told me she'd found it. It wasn't that far away and was full of water, but we retrieved it and cleaned it out and it seemed OK.

Why would someone steal a canoe and then try to sink it? It didn't make sense. Had we made someone mad at us?

Even though we decided to go home the previous night, the fog was lifting and it looked like it was going to be another nice day. We talked about it and finally decided to stay for the day and then leave that evening. We would break camp and get everything put away, enjoy the day, then leave as soon as we got back.

It was about then that we saw something way across the lake, again back near the shore line. We watched for a while but couldn't really make it out until I got out my binoculars, then we again saw the strange heads we were now calling the Gliders for the way they moved without appearing to make any motion. It just seemed really bizarre to us.

I have to concede that Terry has more sense than I do, for she immediately wanted to leave. At that point, we'd pretty much packed everything up except our lunch stuff. Terry had put Barksey on the picnic table to keep him from trying to get in the car.

He kept wanting in, again seeming frantic, but he was too little to jump up, and he would end up under it where we couldn't get to him.

He apparently also saw the figures from being up high enough, because he started whining and whimpering like he had the previous night. Now, if you had a dog that had never made whimpering sounds like that and started doing it while strange things were afoot, wouldn't you take the hint that something's not right? I think most people would, and Terry certainly did, but all I could do was feel angry, thinking this distant pair were responsible for taking our canoe. I actually had the urge to chase after them.

As we watched, they disappeared into the trees along the shore. We quickly finished making our lunches, put everything else in the car, locked it, grabbed Barksey, and headed out in the canoe—I will say against Terry's wishes.

As an aside, in the future, she knows she has top priority in the decision-making process in our family, and I will always concede to her. That was the result from what I stupidly was about to get us into.

Terry was really upset with me, but I insisted on going to the opposite shore where these people or whatever they were had been. I almost feel like I was under the influence of some kind of bravado or something, because I've never been one to look for trouble.

Maybe it was sleep deprivation, or maybe it was everything combined with just enough fear that I lost my common sense.

The closer we get to shore, the more upset Barksey got until he was hiding under my canoe seat. We soon came upon a watercraft. I call it a watercraft because it wasn't a canoe, it was more like a rough-made raft.

Rough logs had been tied together with long strands of what looked like reeds. There wasn't much to it, but it was large and sturdy looking. It made me understand why they wanted a nice canoe, but why had they tried to sink it?

As we pulled up to shore, I saw something that just did not register at the time—huge tracks in the mud all around the raft where the people had gotten out. They were not only huge, but they were also barefoot. It was the strangest thing I've ever seen, and I felt an urge to follow them into the woods.

Later, I described it to myself as feeling like something was taunting me and daring me to come into the trees. Terry was already pushing off from shore with her oar, and that's probably what kept me from getting out. She insisted we go home right then and there, so we started back across the lake.

As we got farther away from the tracks, I began to feel more normal, and I finally ended up being scared to death. I kept looking back, and when we finally reached our camp, I was surprised to see the figures were back again on the raft.

They were now coming across the lake toward our camp. It was no longer misty or foggy at all, and yet they still seemed to glide as if making no motion at all. when Terry realized what was going on she totally freaked out and put Barksey in the car and wanted to leave immediately, but I insisted we put the canoe in its rack and not leave it.

We did this as quickly as possible and when we looked up, the gliders were more than halfway across the lake to our side. We quickly jumped in the car and took off. We passed a number of other campsites, but there was no one anywhere.

We hadn't gone far when Terry started sobbing, and I realized the whole event had traumatized her, probably worse than me. I was actually wrong about it not bothering me, as I started having nightmares not long after that, and it's taken some intensive therapy to get rid of what they're saying is PTSD.

I still don't understand how just seeing something like that can affect one so much, but after reading about other encounters, I think it's safe to say Terry and I aren't the only ones.

Our therapy even involved driving up to Forlorn Lakes one day, but it was kind of a miserable experience, as we both started fixating on what we might see instead of seeing the beauty and all the people there enjoying their day.

That was the only time we've ever been back, and I will say that most people that I've read about stopped enjoying the outdoors after they had an encounter. It's like it really does affect you and your perceptions of the natural world.

After thinking about it a lot, I realized how big the Gliders actually were, and I still don't understand how they moved without seeming to have any motion. Maybe it was because they were so far away, though when they got halfway across the lake where we could make them out better, they were still gliding along.

But Terry thinks they didn't actually try to sink our canoe, but were so big it couldn't hold them and filled with water. Makes sense to me.

We recently gave it to one of her cousins, who was delighted, but we told him to stay away from Forlorn Lakes. He knew our story and agreed it was a good idea.

———

7

IN THE COULEE

Heidi joined my group for a sunny day flyfishing in the Clark Fork River in western Montana, the same river responsible for the huge ice dams she talks about in her story. Of course, the Clark Fork is a small river these days, and the huge ice dams that blocked it many years ago are long gone with the end of the ice ages.

Although her story really has very little to do with the ice dams, they were responsible for the landscape where she had her dangerous and almost fatal encounter. Her story is one everyone should read, for Bigfoot is not always benign and harmless, as she can attest.

—Rusty

I want to start out by saying that I'm just a regular person from a small town in Washington. I don't claim to have any special kind of knowledge, and even after all this happened, I don't feel like I have some kind of unique connection with the unknown.

Actually, I'm not sure Bigfoot really is unknown, it's just that we haven't yet been able to prove it exists. As for my own proof, I personally have all I need. You'll see why in a minute.

I'm a little hesitant to say where this happened, but maybe other people should know in case they want to go there. I have no idea if what I saw is still in the area. Probably not, given that I've talked to a number of people who have hiked this trail and didn't see anything.

Anyway, it was in central Washington at what's called Potholes Coulee. This is actually two coulees that were formed next to each other and have lakes filled with irrigation spill-over water. People fish at the lakes and wildlife comes there to drink—maybe not a lot of wildlife, because it's in what's called the Channeled Scablands, which is very barren country with lots of rattlesnakes. But what I saw there was definitely wild.

At the time, I was having a lot of problems, primarily with the new supervisor at my job. For some reason, he decided to double my workload, and since I was already doing more work than most people there, it got really difficult. I was having trouble keeping up, and I finally realized he was trying to get me fired by saying I couldn't do my job.

I won't go into the details, but I found out later he was a good friend of my ex-husband.

The job was so stressful that I started getting sick from it with headaches and catching everything that went around. Anxiety and stress can do a lot to your health, and I quickly learned that if I wanted to stay healthy, I needed to find a new job.

But the other thing I needed to do was to get out on the weekends and forget everything. I knew from experience that the only way I could really do this was by getting out of town and into nature. So I started hiking every weekend.

Well, one week at work went particularly bad, so I decided to get far away for the weekend. I really wanted to get away from people, so I decided to stay out of the nearby mountains. The Channeled Scablands weren't that far and there's some nice camping down by the Columbia Gorge, so I decided to head that direction.

I remembered someone talking about fishing in Potholes Coulee, so I checked out the main trail into the upper coulee, which is called the Dusty Lake Trail. The trail seemed to be well-known and even had a parking lot at its head, but it was early March, so I didn't expect to see very many people.

The Dusty Lake Trail is what most people would call primitive. In fact, there are places where you can take a tumble if you're not paying attention. It basically cuts through basalt with lots of big rocks, and even though it doesn't have very much up and down, there are a few places where you have to really watch your step.

I figured I'd go to the first lake on the far side, opposite from the trail, and set up a little camp there behind some rocks where nobody could see me. I would be out of the wind, plus I could just enjoy the solitude and quiet, for even if people came on the trail they would be on the other side of the lake.

After all this happened, I tried to research if anything similar had happened to anyone else. I talked to a lot of people, but nobody knew anything. This was before all the reports on the Internet were a thing. Maybe this creature was on its way through and just didn't like me being there, I don't know.

I will say that the Channeled Scablands are the last place I expect to see a Bigfoot. If you've never flown over eastern Washington, this whole area looks like the moon. From an airplane, you would see a jumble of huge areas of basalt with deep canyons cut in various places.

Millions of years ago, the region had huge lava flows that flooded the entire Columbia Basin, creating basalt layers thousands of feet thick, and the coulees were cut through this basalt. How did this happen?

If you study them for a moment, you'll notice that these channels aren't V-shaped like a valley would be, but are U-shaped with no creeks or rivers cutting through them. People wondered for years how they were formed, though some thought it was from glaciers cutting through the rock.

I know I'm getting off topic, but this was part of why I ended up on the Dusty Lake Trail—I wanted to see these coulees and learn more about them, because the way they were formed is one of the most amazing stories I've ever heard.

During the last Ice Age, some 10,000 to 20,000 years ago, part of a glacier blocked the Clark Fork River over in northern Idaho. This river normally flowed into Washington near Spokane. This created an ice dam that caused the river to form a huge lake called Glacial Lake Missoula, and you can see the giant ripple marks on the hills around that town.

It eventually covered 3,000 square miles, containing as much water as Lake Erie and Lake Ontario combined. The ice dam broke, creating one of the largest floods in the history of the world. NASA satellite imagery shows the network of channels carved out by the mega floods, which are these coulees I was talking about.

Water hundreds of feet deep washed away everything in the path in a matter of days, and at their peak flow the floodwaters were around 800 feet deep. The large boulders you see dropped on the basalt were glacial erratics, rocks carried on the floating icebergs and dropped here and there.

The topsoil was carried away, and the floodwaters scoured thousands of square miles of basalt bedrock and created the coulees. Geologists believe that this cycle of an ice dam forming and holding back waters then breaking happened more than 40 times.

Over 150 distinct coulees or long channels were cut into the bedrock, some hundreds of feet deep. The two largest are Moses Coulee, which is 40 miles long, and Grand Coulee, which is 60 miles long.

The bottom of these coulees are a rugged mess of rocks, unlike valleys formed by rivers. These rocks have a part in my story, which I'll now get back to. Sorry for the diversion, but it seems important to understand the landscape, because some of these rocks played a part in the danger I found myself in.

OK, It was a nice sunny Saturday in March when I threw my stuff in my car and headed out. It wasn't real far to the trailhead, and when I got there it was still early. Mine was the only car there.

I put on my backpack, which was fairly light because all it had was my small backpacking tent, my sleeping bag, enough food for a couple of days, and my small kerosene stove. I carried water jugs tied to my pack, but I also had a filter, even though I didn't want to use it, knowing there's a lot of chemicals in irrigation water, which was what fed the lakes.

I remember heading down the trail and thinking about all the real backpacking trips I'd been on in places like Yellowstone and the Tetons. These had been serious trips of a week or two, where you're in the middle of nowhere. I always went alone and loved it. The only dangers were myself making a mistake, like mis-stepping and breaking an ankle or a close encounter with a bear or mountain lion.

Even though it was early March, it felt like it was going to get pretty warm. I wondered if the rattlesnakes might be coming out early because this was definitely snake territory. I felt pretty lucky, though, because there was no wind, which was really unusual for March. I knew it wouldn't last, because the forecast called for wind with a possible storm coming in a few days.

I took my time down the trail, kind of lollygagging, as it was only a couple miles down to the lake, really enjoying myself, far from my job. Once I got to the head of the lake, I started along the left side, where I had to make my own trail.

It took a lot longer to make headway, as there were plenty of big boulders, but I was in no hurry. I was weaving in and out and over these rocks that littered the coulee. I kept glancing over at the other side of the lake where the main trail was, wondering if I would see anybody, but I never did.

At one point, I stopped on a big flat piece of basalt and pulled out a couple of granola bars and some water. I had started thinking about my job again, and I sat there, trying to shake off the bad feelings. And at that very moment, something broke in my mind, something big, because I suddenly felt lighthearted, like nothing mattered.

I somehow knew that when I got back everything would be all right. The reason I knew everything would be all right was because at that very moment I decided to quit. I had enough in savings to last for a while, and working in a grocery store is not a really skilled job, so I knew I could find something else.

I don't know why I decided then and there to quit my job, but I suddenly felt a sense of euphoria. I almost got up and did a jig. I just remember being very happy for the first time in quite a long time.

Does Bigfoot sense emotions? Is it possible that the creature was nearby and sensed how happy I was? It doesn't seem very likely to me, but if so, it had also surely sensed how unhappy I was coming down the trail. I guess I'm just trying to figure out what had set it off. It was probably territorial and just didn't like people.

So, I sat there feeling what I'll call blissful because that kind of explains that type of irrational feeling. It went way beyond just quitting my job, it was more like I'd won the lottery.

I finally got up and kept on hiking, still taking my time, until I came to what looked like the perfect place for a small tent. It was behind a large rock, and there were large rocks above it so you couldn't see down into it from the hillside.

I sat there again for awhile trying to get a feel for the place, suddenly wondering if I really even wanted to spend the night. I could just go home and be happy. But then the more I thought about it, the more I worried that if I got home and was surrounded by familiar things, like the pile of bills on my desk, I would change my mind again and not quit.

So, I set up camp just in time for the winds to start in. If there's one thing I hate when camping, it's the wind. It's ever-present and you can't get away, and it will slowly drive you crazy, especially the howling kind, which this was. It seemed to get stiffer as the day went on until I had to put large rocks on the corners of my tent so it wouldn't blow away.

A friend of mine has a saying—float with the wind. She says this when she knows I need to relax. Float with the wind. Well if I had floated with that wind, I would've ended up in Idaho or Montana.

I don't know where the day went, but I do know I spent some of it hiding out in my tent. There was a spectacular sunset, partly because a few clouds from the oncoming storm had come in, and there was lots of dust in the air, turning everything a brilliant ruby color. It was a truly dazzling sight, and I smiled, telling myself it was worth everything just to see the sunset.

It got dark really quickly, and I sat outside of my tent for a while, back against the wind behind a large rock, just watching as the earth turned and everything went to sleep. I could hear the waves of the lake lapping against the shore. Finally, the stars came out, and I realized that they weren't going to be very spectacular because of all the dust.

I waited until it was totally dark, but the stars weren't very bright, so crawled inside my tent. I would listen to a podcast I'd downloaded back home on my tablet. I got into my pajamas and crawled into my sleeping bag. I put on my headphones and turned the volume way down.

Even though no one else could hear it, I was wary of making noise, as when I'm out alone I don't like to be seen nor heard, and I often hike off-trail. I think it's a preservation tactic from being a woman hiking solo.

I had just settled in and was listening to a podcast about the national parks when I felt a surge of panic go through me, telling me to turn off the sound.

I turned everything off, took off my headphones, and was very still, listening. Why had I felt so panicked? Was my intuition telling me there must be something outside? I was totally quiet when I heard a sound way in the distance, over toward the lower coulee.

I can't really describe the sound except to say it was like a jake-brake on a truck, that deep sound of compressed air being released from exhaust valves. Interstate 90 was a good 10 miles away in the direction it was coming from, but I was puzzled how one could hear it that far, especially over the noisy wind.

I eventually went to sleep, and when I awoke, the tent walls were glowing red from the sunrise, which was red from all the dust. If anything, the wind was worse. I'm amazed I got any sleep at all, with my nylon tent snapping.

I stuck my head out and looked around, but it was still dark enough all I could really see was the shapes of all the rocks around me. The lake wasn't in sight at all. Imagine my surprise when I thought I saw one of the big rocks moving!

I closed my eyes for a second and when I opened them, the rock was completely gone. Well, that gave me pause, for sure. I decided I must still be half-asleep, but when I looked outside again, the rock was still gone. It had to have been a dream that it was ever there in the first place.

That day, the winds picked up, and there were dark clouds coming in. I wasn't worried, because it was warm enough all it would do is rain, and it wasn't supposed to come in for a couple more days.

I made some freeze-dried eggs for breakfast, along with some coffee, then tidied everything up. For a moment, I had the urge to pick up camp and leave, but then I thought about my job and how nice it was to be away from everything, and I decided to stick with my initial plan and stay.

I would enjoy one more day of solitude, then go home and deal with giving my notice and quitting my job. I could deal with the rain, as my tent was rainproof.

I was leaning against a rock, wondering if I should give them two weeks' notice or just leave, when I caught something out of the corner of my eye. I wouldn't have been surprised to see people out there, as it was a well-used tail, but to see anyone over on my side of the lake would be a surprise. It just wasn't a place one would casually stroll over to, with all the rocks everywhere.

There was nothing there, so I decided it had to either be my imagination or else a marmot or gopher. It was about then that I saw a pair of bald eagles circling high above, so I excitedly got out my camera gear. It would be fun to take some photos and see if I could get a good video.

There was a ridge between where I was and the second coulee. Keep in mind that these are large coulees, and the ridge was at least a mile or two away. The eagles flew over by it, and as I watched, I could see something standing on the ridge's crest.

At first I thought it was a person, but then I realized how big it had to be. I put on my telephone lens and could see what looked like a large figure. Judging by nearby bushes, it looked to be at least eight or 10 feet tall. No defining features could be seen, except a hat or crest on the top of its head.

Once I realized how large this thing was, I watched it through my telephoto, trying to figure it out. The more I watched, the more chilled I became. Soon it went straight up the side of the rugged coulee, and I knew the red flags I'd been feeling weren't my imagination. As I watched this large being climb straight up the side of what looked like unclimbable cliffs, it seemed totally unbelievable.

It was soon gone, and I focused again on the eagles, who were now much closer. I don't know how, but I kind of forgot about the figure, now enthralled with the eagles as they circled close above me.

I have some beautiful photos from that day of two eagles spiraling against a blue sky that I never show anyone, as they make me anxious. They are forever linked in my mind with that intimidating being I saw right before. I think disregarding it was my way of dealing with something I didn't understand or believe could be real.

It was soon time for lunch. I made a sandwich, then got really sleepy, crawled in my tent and took long nap, regardless of the howling winds. I woke once again feeling anxious, and the thought occurred to me that I really should get out of there.

I decided it was my intuition telling me the storm was coming in early and I should leave.

I've read a lot of Bigfoot encounters since then, and in a lot of them, their intuition or sixth sense tells them to leave, and they ignore it and get in trouble. But at that point, I remembered a dream I'd had the previous night. I had completely forgotten about it until then, but it came back in full force.

I was dreaming about my grandfather, who lived next door to us when I was a kid. After he retired, he would come over every morning for coffee with my mom. He never said much to me, in fact, I don't remember him talking to me at all other than to say hello.

He wasn't one of those grandfatherly types who was always giving you advice, but was instead a man of few words. I think it was because he had worked outdoors all his life and was used to being alone. Anyway, in my dream, my grandfather had taken me aside and was telling me I needed to listen to my intuition because it would tell me when I was in danger.

We were standing at the mouth of a small cave, and I was getting ready to go inside and explore it. It was an odd dream for me, because I don't like caves. I remember telling him I agreed, and then the cave disappeared. The dream was simple, but it left me with a feeling that all was not right.

Once I was awake, I was feeling like I should leave, so, unlike a lot of people who have encounters, I listened to my intuition and put everything away. I wasn't having that much fun, there was a storm coming in, and I'd seen the dark figure, and even though it was a couple of miles away, it seemed ominous, so it was time to go.

I slipped my backpack on and started back through all the rocks. For some reason it seemed much more tedious than coming in, probably because I wasn't excited any longer.

I had to be careful because basalt will really rip you up if you fall on it, as it has a really rugged surface. That side of the lake was up against the cliffs, so as I was making my way, I remember thinking it would be a good place to ambush someone, because there were rocks above me one could easily push down.

I had no longer thought it when it happened—a bunch of rocks came down, barely missing me. If they had hit me, I would've been killed.

I sat for a moment, shaken up, looking up above me to see if more rocks were going to come down, then I threaded my way through the new rockfall. I was really happy when I got around that side of the lake and reached the trail. I felt a sense of relief and headed toward the parking lot.

At one point, I turned around to look behind me to get one last view of the lake, and what I saw terrified me. That dark figure was coming my way along the trail and it truly was huge, and it wasn't all that far away.

It was making good time because it was so large and so big, and it wouldn't be long before it caught up to me. I wanted to run, but my pack was too heavy and cumbersome, but I upped the pace and was walking as fast as I could.

From nowhere, a large rock landed in front of me with a clunk, right at my feet, barely missing me. Now another two or three came in. They missed but were very close. I didn't know what to do, because I was going as fast as I could, but I was ready to ditch my pack.

Whatever it was, it had to be large to be able to throw rocks that big, and it was wily, because now when I turned back, it wasn't there.

The next thing I knew, I was falling to the ground. A large rock had hit me square in the back of my head and knocked me off my feet. The last thing I remember is the sound of voices as I passed out.

When I woke up, I was in the hospital, but it took me some time to figure out where I was. My head was bandaged, and I had an IV in my arm. A nurse was sitting there checking my blood pressure and asking me how I was. I remember she buzzed the doctor because she was so excited.

Apparently, when I come to it was a big deal because I was in a coma from a major concussion. I had been out for a couple of days.

I was soon home, where the first thing I did was to call my job to tell them why I had missed work. It's kind of funny the way it worked out, because I was worried about my manager being mad at me, even though I was still going to quit, but he didn't even let me tell him why I'd been gone, he just fired me on the spot. This meant I qualified for unemployment, which was an unexpected bonus.

The voices I'd heard after the rock hit me was a group of people coming down the trail who fortunately found me and took me to the hospital. I still have no idea who any of them were. I would like to ask them if they saw the big black creature, but I guess that will always be a mystery.

At one point I drove back out to the trailhead, and I remember standing by my car looking down toward the Columbia Gorge and feeling a sense of anxiety and that I needed to get out of there immediately.

I haven't been out in the scablands since then. In fact, after I left my job, I enjoyed a long vacation, then got a job with a local doctors' clinic submitting forms to Medicare for reimbursement. It's kind of boring, but since I work at home, I can live wherever I want.

Right now I live in Leavenworth, which I like a lot, so I'll probably stay here. There are some spectacular mountains nearby, but I haven't been out to visit them other than just driving around in my car.

I've kind of lost my taste for backpacking. I know the thing that threw the rock was a Bigfoot, because there's nothing else out there big enough to throw something like that. I'm at peace with it, since I'll never go back.

I hope others follow their intuition if anything similar happens to them, because in spite of what people say, I don't believe Bigfoot is always peaceful. I think some are very dangerous, and I have a scar on the back of my head to prove it.

———

8

VOLCANOES, GOATS, AND BIGFOOT

One of my wife's best friends invited us to her wedding over in Salt Lake City, and we were happy to be able to attend. It was held in a beautiful park, and since I didn't really know any of Sarah's college friends, I was kind of hiding out by the food table during the reception.

I must've looked out of place, because the fellow filming the wedding came up and struck up a conversation, probably because he, too, didn't know anyone. His name was Shawn, and he apparently had read some of my books, because he recognized my name.

Since the wedding was over and his duties were fulfilled, he told me he had a story he would like to tell. I got my recorder, and we sat down under a big tree, where he told the following.

—Rusty

My story is pretty straightforward, though I wish I could fully understand exactly what happened. I probably never will, and maybe it's for the best. I'm pretty sure that what we were dealing with was a Bigfoot, but I'm not sure I want to believe in them.

It all started when my best friend, Jeremy, invited me to go stay at his aunt and uncle's farm for a few weeks. It was the end of summer, and they were going to a wedding in Poland, combining it with a vacation.

They were originally from Poland and had tons of family they hadn't seen for years, so it was a big deal for them. They had animals that needed daily care, so Jeremy was going to go and take care of their farm.

At first, I was eager to go, as the farm was in the Puyallup region of Washington, a beautiful pastoral area with scenic hills and incredible berries and flowers, named for the Puyallup Tribe. But when I found out what my part of the farm caretaking would be, I wasn't so eager.

Puyallup's at the foot of Mount Rainier and about 35 miles south of Seattle, where Jeremy and I both worked at the same bank. Puyallup is also known as being the site of the Washington State Fair and Daffodil Festival.

Jeremy's family grew hops and barley for breweries, as well as having some stands of berry bushes. In addition, Jeremy's Aunt Rose had a small business selling goat milk, as well as making goat milk soaps and lotions, so she had a small herd of some kind of goats—I think she said they were Alpines. I don't know much about goats, but these were extremely tame and friendly.

Part of why we were needed was to milk them, as they couldn't be neglected or they would dry up. She had regular customers who would come every day to buy the milk, some of which were natural foods grocers around the region. I think she did pretty well financially.

This was the part of the deal I wasn't so eager to do, milk those darn goats. Jeremy was getting paid to do it, and he generously offered to split the money with me if I'd help milk. I'm a city boy, having grown up in an apartment in the heart of Cincinnati, and I'd never milked anything in my life except maybe my parents when I was a kid and wanted spending money.

We finally came to an agreement—I would work for free if he'd do all the milking. My part would be to feed and help with customers. I didn't mind doing that, as it was hands-off when it came to animals. I'd never even had a dog or cat, so I was kind of intimidated. Oh, and they also had two Border Collies, but I soon learned to get along with them.

We would be there for two weeks. In retrospect, they were the best two weeks of my life in some ways, and also, though not the worst days of my life, right up there. We'd both managed to get the time off, which should've been a red flag that our services at the bank weren't very necessary. We found that out when we returned to work and they let us both go.

Let me describe the farm a little. They had several large strawberry, blackberry, and raspberry patches. All but the blackberries had already ripened and been harvested, and the blackberries were close. Aunt Rose told us to be sure the goats didn't get into the berry patches, which were fenced.

The rest of the farm consisted of several hundred acres of hops and barley, which were ripening, since it was late summer. They were nearly ready for harvest, the stalks turning a beautiful amber gold. I have some really nice photos I took there, with the fields all golden and a distant Mount Rainier in the background.

As for Mount Rainier, let me mention a few things about it, as it ended up having a role in the story. I'm sure you know it's an active volcano, but what most people don't know is that it's been very destructive at times in the past, but not necessarily from fire and falling ash, like Mount Saint Helens.

Instead, Mount Rainier has had at least three huge lahar flows in the past 10,000 years, the most recent being some 500 years ago. What's a lahar? It's basically a big mudflow, the result of a volcanic eruption that mixes lava with glacial ice and loose rocks and sediments from the slopes of the mountain.

Lahars can reach 100 feet in height and travel 45 to 50 miles per hour. They can occur without warning, and a lahar from Mount Rainier would reach populated areas within an hour. They're like flowing concrete, and they destroy or bury everything in their path. The most recent lahar covered everything in 500 feet of debris.

Deposits of past lahars cover all the valleys that drain from Mount

Rainier's summit, which is basically the entire area around the mountain. These flows have gone all the way to Puget Sound. In addition, the mountain has mudflows from rains every spring and fall, though these generally only affect areas within the boundaries of Mount Rainier National Park.

OK, I'm sure, if you know where Puyallup is, you can guess that it's right smack in the path of a lahar. It's downstream of the western flank of Mount Rainier, which has the highest potential for producing massive landslides, and the entire valley is built on thick deposits of the 5,600-year-old Osceola Mudflow, an example of one of the largest lahars Mount Rainier could produce.

Should Mount Rainier erupt, everyone in the valley will need to evacuate to higher ground. The county has set up a lahar warning system, which they test on the first Monday of each month. A bunch of sirens go off, making a big racket, along with verbal and flashing warnings.

OK, now back to our foray into animal husbandry. On our way down to the farm, Jeremy made a casual comment about his aunt being pretty nuts. I wasn't sure what to make of it, so I asked why he thought that.

He replied, "She's tried for years to talk Uncle Mark into selling the farm. She's deathly afraid of dying from a lahar. Apparently, when she was young, she had a vivid dream that she was in an avalanche, trying to escape. It must've really scared her, and the older she gets the more scared she seems to be. She won't even go into the mountains any more.

Honestly, the odds of her dying in a plane crash on her way to Poland are higher, and they're still pretty low. Oh, and I asked her one time to describe the dream, and the avalanche was white, all snow, not like a lahar would be."

"How would a lahar be?" I asked, knowing he knew about as much about them as I did, which was nothing.

"Not white. Maybe ash-colored, but not white like snow. But what's really crazy is she has a truck and stock trailer sitting ready to go in case there is a lahar."

"Maybe a bit paranoid," I replied. "But not really crazy."

"Maybe not," Jeremy countered. "But she has all her goats trained to run into it when they hear those dang sirens. Once a month during the emergency test, they all run into the stock trailer, then she has to go coax them out. They're scared, and she's trained them to feel that way. Sometimes, when an ambulance or police car comes by with their siren, they run into the trailer. You have to go coax them out with food, or they just stay in there."

"Kind of a pain," I said. "But if there ever is a lahar, she'll be glad she trained them."

We stopped at an espresso place called Bigfoot Java, and the conversation drifted to Bigfoot, a popular topic anywhere in Washington.

Jeremy had no idea if Bigfoot had ever been sighted around Puyallup, but he knew they had been seen around Mount Rainier. He went on to say that all the valleys under the mountain were incredibly rich volcanic soil, and it wouldn't surprise him one bit if Bigfoot didn't sneak down from the wilds to partake of the delicious berries and other crops. When I said it sounded like he really believed in them, he said he wasn't sure.

Well, when we got there, I found Jeremy's Aunt Rose to be a really nice person, and she gave him a full hands-on lesson in goat milking before they left. She was really adamant that we not forget to put the goats in at night, saying there were "things" that would get them. There were eight goats, and she left us a list she'd made of their names—names like Popcorn, Pickles, and Pumpkin.

We were soon up to our elbows in taking care of a herd of goats and two dogs, though the dogs were easy. I was kind of amazed at how the goats would stand while being milked and butt each other out of the way to be next, but when she said being full of milk could get uncomfortable, I understood and made sure I would remind Jeremy of his duties there if he slacked off.

I knew from working with him at the bank that he was good at procrastinating. If you didn't milk them regularly, they would dry up, she said, and it would only take a week. That would be a disaster for her business.

She also said it would take a couple of hours to milk them, and it should be done twice daily, but she was going to have him just do it in the mornings while they were gone. The goats would end up producing less milk, but she could get them back on schedule when they returned.

They left, and our first afternoon there was really nice. We explored the farm, walking around the fields and down to the nearby Puyallup River. There was an amazing sunset, and I helped Jeremy put the goats to bed in the nearby barn, where they were herded each night. This was mostly to keep them out of trouble, but also because there were occasional predators around, as the riverway seemed to be a sort of highway for wildlife.

That night, we barbecued hotdogs out on their back deck, deciding that a foray into town the next day would include getting lots of stuff we could grill. We shared an apartment back in Seattle, and sitting outside eating food we'd just cooked was a real treat, kind of like a picnic.

The dogs each got a hotdog, then we settled back, watching the sunset and enjoying our good luck at being there. As it got dark, the dogs wanted inside, which I thought was just normal behavior, not knowing dogs. But Jeremy said it was unusual, as dogs like to be with their people. And the longer we were out, the more they wanted in, until we finally put them inside, where they sat by the screen door watching us, ears forward like they were looking for something.

We finally put everything away and decided to go inside. For some reason, I thought it would be a good idea to check on the goats one last time before going to bed. I'm pretty conscientious, almost to a fault, and I wanted to sleep peacefully, knowing they were OK.

I slipped over to the barn, looking through a crack in the door, and saw that everything was fine, the goats happily munching their hay. I told them goodnight and how we were going to take good care of them and then went back to the house.

I've noticed this in people not used to being around animals—

you tend to talk to them as if they can understand you, I mean in complete sentences. The first time I wanted them in the barn, I tried to talk them into coming inside, and I even tried pushing a couple of them in, which was an exercise in futility. Jeremy said I had to put their feed inside, then they would come in on their own. You entice them, not try to physically force them.

The farm had a big halogen light that lit up the space between the house and barn, which made it feel secure. Back inside, we talked a little about how different it was from our apartment, and then decided it was time for bed. Jeremy got the master bedroom, and I slept in the guest room on the other side of the house. I could see the drive and barn, whereas he couldn't.

In fact, I could see the barn when I was in bed, as long as I left the curtain open. The dogs both slept with Jeremy, as that was where they were used to sleeping with his aunt and uncle. I remember dozing off, watching the barn through the window, wishing one of the dogs would sleep with me as it felt a little spooky way out there in the country. I was used to traffic noise and people talking in the halls of our apartment.

I slept well, though I did wake a couple of times. The next morning I had to get Jeremy up and around to milk. I ended up making coffee and then breakfast while he took his sweet time showering and getting dressed. He finally started the milking while I looked on and helped as best I could.

His aunt had showed us how to prepare the milk for her customers, and they were soon arriving. It was a really busy morning, and I was regretting telling him I would work for nothing. By afternoon, we were free to do whatever we wanted, which included going into town for groceries and ice cream.

We were still in town when the sirens went off. I panicked and started running to the car, but when I saw everyone else ignoring them, I knew it was the monthly test day. The sirens made a real racket, getting the adrenaline pumping, and I was glad I lived in Seattle where lahars aren't a concern, just earthquakes.

Back on the farm, I noticed the dogs seemed really happy to see us, but I figured that was normal until Jeremy said they were panting like they were worried about something. He's always had dogs, so is more aware of their behavior. They kept going over to the stock trailer, which was parked in the drive by the barn. That's when we realized the goats had loaded themselves up and were still in there. They'd heard the sirens and done what they were trained to do.

They jumped right out when we walked over there and shushed them out, then they went about their normal day. We were relieved, as we hadn't known how they would act when the sirens went off, and now we didn't have to worry about it any more, as it was only a monthly thing.

Well, it was evening, and I fed the dogs and got the grill going, this time with hamburgers. We would have macaroni salad and a bunch of other picnic stuff, eating high on the hog. Thinking about this later, I think all our grilling was partly what attracted our visitors, but I'm getting ahead of myself.

Jeremy herded the goats into the barn, giving them their hay and grain, saying they wanted to be milked and wondering if he shouldn't go ahead with it, even though his aunt said he didn't have to.

I knew he wouldn't do it, as he's a slacker, which he freely admits. I thought about doing it myself, then realized I would probably end up having to do all the milking, both morning and evening, because he's good at convincing me to do things. This is partly why we're so compatible and are good friends. I'm OK with it, as he makes up for it in other ways, like putting up with my ongoing anxiety.

Everything went smoothly for the first week we were there, with us enjoying their barbecue grill and the farm in general. We would often go exploring during the day after the goats were milked, driving up into Mount Rainier National Park and also over to the ocean.

In all honesty, it was kind of like a farm stay where you pay to live like a local, and we probably should've been paying his aunt and uncle instead of them paying us. Some of the blackberries had ripened, so we also enjoyed picking and eating them right off the bushes.

I always counted the goats when we put them in the barn, just to be sure. I clearly recall counting them that particular night, and they were all there. We again fired up the grill, this time having brats, and I remember telling Jeremy we were eating too much meat. It wasn't good for us, plus it was getting real expensive. He laughed and said we could always have some goat meat, which I didn't find funny at all.

So when Jeremy was milking and said there was a goat missing, I thought he was just kidding along the lines of us eating goat meat, like he'd killed one. I told him it wasn't funny, and he said it wasn't meant to be, that a goat *was* missing, and he thought it was Pumpkin, as she had odd markings on her face, making her easy to recognize.

I thought back to the previous night when the dogs had come into my room around 2 a.m. and jumped up on my bed, growling and carrying on, looking out the window. When I realized what was going on, I also looked, and I saw a shadow quickly disappear behind the barn.

I figured it was a coyote or something and made the dogs leave, closing my door. I could hear them by the door whining most of the night, but I managed to sleep off and on, anyway, but found it strange they didn't want to go sleep with Jeremy.

I told Jeremy, and he said we should keep our eye on the goats that day and not go anywhere, as a mountain lion or something could be around, hiding down by the river.

We scoured the farm looking for Pumpkin, and that's when we discovered that something had pretty much demolished the blackberries, stripping the berries off the bushes.

Finally, we found her—she'd been hiding in the stock trailer. She was skittish and wanted back in the barn, so we took her inside, Jeremy milked her, then we tried to get her to go outside, but she wouldn't budge. She even tried to kick Jeremy, which was unheard of.

It then dawned on me that the entire herd had wanted to stay in the barn that morning. Jeremy had asked me to come help him get them out after milking, which was a first, as they generally loved being outside.

We then tried to figure out how Pumpkin had gotten out. There had to be a hole or something she could slip through, but we found nothing. This left one solution—someone had taken her out. She would've never gone out on her own at night without the others.

I then remembered the dogs coming into my room and told Jeremy. Someone had definitely been there, maybe trying to steal the goats!

We were in a pickle. We didn't want to worry Jeremy's aunt and uncle, as we knew they'd come back early. We were enjoying our time there, but we also didn't want anything to happen to the goats.

We went into town and bought a big strong lock for the barn door, as well as a couple of motion-sensor lights. I'm not sure how we thought lights would wake us, especially out in the barn, but maybe they would deter a thief.

I then decided we needed a camera to see what was going on, so we bought one of those cameras you put in your baby's room. We found out later it didn't have enough signal to reach from the barn to the house.

That night, all seemed well, the goats were settled, and we went to bed, tired, the dogs back to sleeping with Jeremy. I told him I would wake him if they came into my room. Well, sure enough, we were both awakened during the night, but it wasn't from the dogs, it was from the horrible screaming coming from the barn.

I looked out the window, barely awake, just in time to see something big and dark coming around the side of the barn, and it looked like it was carrying a goat, who was bleating and crying for all it was worth.

I yelled for Jeremy as I ran for the back door, the dogs at my feet. They were outside chasing before I could stop them, and the dark figure was gone, still carrying a goat, never stepping into the light from the big halogen lamp.

The dogs were going down toward the river, barking for all they were worth, Jeremy now up and calling them. We both ran for the barn, where we found the rest of the goats hunched up together in a far corner, trying to hide. The lock on the door hadn't been touched, the door instead having been wrenched off its hinges and tossed a good 10 feet away.

Yikes! Jeremy and I were both dumbfounded. I described what I saw as we both continued calling the dogs. I worried we would never see them again, but they returned before long, panting, their tongues hanging out, totally spent. They wanted in the house so badly they started biting the door, which they never did.

I let them in, asking Jeremy if his relatives had a shotgun or anything, even though I didn't know how to use one. Surely they'd had to defend their livestock before. He explained that once the goats were in the barn, they were totally safe, as coyotes and lions couldn't get inside. Maybe a bear could if it was really strong, but he'd never heard of bears coming around.

We fixed the door, rehanging it on its hinges, and by then it was dawn. We wouldn't have been able to sleep, anyway, especially after we found the huge tracks by the barn. We both knew we were dealing with Bigfoot, yet we weren't sure we believed in them. Maybe it was just some big guy who'd made fake tracks to throw everyone off when he stole things. And why did he want a goat? For its milk?

We both knew the answer, and it wasn't a very pleasant thought, especially when we figured out it was Cocoa, one of our favorites. It didn't help matters when we discovered blood on one of the dogs.

Well, I can say that we both just wanted to go back to Seattle at that point, barbecues and exploring the countryside be darned. How would we explain to Aunt Rose that one of her prized goats had been stolen?

We couldn't afford to lose another goat, but what could we do? Jeremy set to milking while I made breakfast, trying to make sense of what I'd seen, but with no luck. We spent most of the day beside ourselves, trying to figure out how to protect the goats during the coming night. Should we take turns standing guard?

In the meantime, the dogs had wanted nothing to do with being outdoors, basically following Jeremy around when he was in the house, shaking and whining. I managed to get the blood off the one, Tommy, and I noted it had a really odd odor to it, more like a skunk than blood would smell. It also had a greenish tint, which I found strange.

We still hadn't solved how to protect the goats when I saw something climbing up the hill from the riverway below us. It was black, and seemed to be limping. I at first thought it was a deer, but I knew deer are never black. I could finally make out that it was goat. It was Cocoa!

She went straight into the stock trailer, and we ran out there. She had some scratches on her, and her leg seemed to be twisted, and I knew it had to be from where the Bigfoot had grabbed her. And she had some of that strange blood on her. Had the dogs struggled with the Bigfoot, injuring it, and she'd gotten away and hidden until now?

She needed medical care, so Jeremy closed the trailer up and drove the pickup and trailer straight to the vet while I stayed and kept an eye on things. While he was gone, a way to keep the goats safe came to me—we could put them in the stock trailer and lock it. It was big enough for the goats to spend the night in comfort if we put some hay down for them to lay on.

Proud of my analytic abilities, I started dinner, once more on the grill, but this time chicken shish kabobs. When Jeremy got back, we spread hay on the floor of the trailer, making it soft, then hung water buckets along the sides where they couldn't spill them.

Once the trailer was ready, Jeremy decided to park it by the house, smack dab at the back door where we could keep a close eye on things. We wondered if his aunt had ever dealt with Bigfoot, but Jeremy doubted it, figuring it would've tipped her over the edge and she would've insisted they sell out and leave.

We now had a new problem—the darn goats wouldn't get in the trailer. It's like they sensed something was wrong. Maybe they sensed something had happened to Cocoa, as Jeremy had left her at the vet clinic for treatment for pulled ligaments. We tried to coax them in with grain, but they were totally gun shy, like it had hot lava on the floor.

We were about to give up and just put them back in the barn when an ambulance went by and they all hopped in upon hearing the siren. We quickly closed the back door, laughing at our luck while hoping whoever was in the ambulance would be OK. Their misfortune was our luck, 'cause we could now go inside and go to bed.

I will admit to being scared that night. I slept with the curtain pulled across the window looking out to the barn, but I could still see a couple of times when the motion lights went on. There was something out there, but I didn't want to go see what it was.

Actually, I didn't need to go see because it told me in no uncertain terms with an incredible scream that shook the house. It was actually a combination scream/howl, unlike anything I've ever heard, and I hope to never hear it again.

It curdled my blood and made my hair stand on end, and I'll never forget it. It was followed by the dogs barking and then the sound of the goats bleating and crying out.

I jumped up and ran to the back door, where I could see the stock trailer. The dogs were at my feet, wanting out, but there was no way I was going to risk them getting hurt or maybe worse. The stock trailer was lit up by the halogen light, and I could easily see a large black figure trying to wrench the back door off the trailer with long muscular arms.

Jeremy was soon beside me, and we both knew we had just a few minutes to act before it got to the goats. But what could we do? We didn't have any kind of arms or any way to scare it off.

I grabbed the pickup keys from the hanger by the door and slipped outside, making sure the dogs stayed in, then ran for the cab, which wasn't more than 20 feet away. The Bigfoot must not have seen me, for it was still trying to wrench off the back gate to the trailer.

I fired up the truck and peeled out, the trailer jerking so hard I thought for a minute it would come unhitched. I know I probably knocked all the goats off their feet. I was soon rolling down the highway, trying to get a feel for the rig, as I'd never pulled a trailer before and had hardly even driven a pickup. If it hadn't been an automatic, I would still have it in first gear.

Later, when everything settled down, Jeremy told me the Bigfoot rode along on the bumper for a bit, then swung down onto the ground, tumbling head over heel from the speed, though it didn't look injured.

I was now on the highway to town, not sure where I was going, and also not sure if the Bigfoot was riding along with me or not. I couldn't see the back to tell if it was hanging on or not. I knew I had to get someplace safe, where I could hang out with the goats for awhile until Jeremy or someone helped me out.

Like I mentioned earlier, Puyallup is the home to the Washington State Fair, which attracts over a million people, or so they say. The fairgrounds are extensive, and the town has actually grown around them, with different gates for different sectors. Being a fairgrounds, it has barns and corrals for stock, and I somehow managed to find some small pens, where I stopped, ignoring the no overnight parking signs.

It was pitch dark, but I was able to get a quick look at the goats through the trailer slats using my phone light and could see they seemed to be OK. I turned off the truck, got back into the cab, and tried to call Jeremy on my cell phone.

There was no answer, and I spent the rest of the night worrying that something had happened to him and the dogs. I thought about calling the sheriff's office, then decided they would just say I was crazy and maybe even give me a ticket for overnight parking at the fairgrounds.

Finally, the next morning, I heard from Jeremy. He had taken the dogs and fled the farm, getting a motel room, leaving his phone behind, he was in such a hurry. He was back on the farm. Could I bring the goats back for milking? All Rose's clients would be showing up soon for milk.

I laughed at the situation. We were both scared to death, running on fumes, and yet we had to milk the goats or they would be miserable. I fired up the truck and headed back to the farm.

Once there, the goats refused to get out, so Jeremy had to milk them in the trailer. I helped as much as I could, keeping them out of his way as much as possible while he was milking.

Once done, we pondered what we should do. We walked all

around the barn, trying to think of a way we could keep the goats safe, but having seen the size of the Bigfoot, which we were now pretty sure was what we'd seen, we knew it was impossible. Would it return again? We had no idea, but we couldn't risk it. Besides, neither of us wanted to be around if it came back.

I got on the phone with the fairgrounds management and rented a corral with a small shelter. We would just keep the goats there until Rose returned. We could park the stock trailer by the pen and camp out in it at night, then milk the goats and take turns keeping an eye on them during the day. It would only be a for a few more days.

It didn't take long to gather up some grain and hay and take the goats back down to the fairgrounds, along with the dogs and some camping gear. We kind of looked at it as an adventure, and sleeping in the trailer wasn't too bad. Jeremy would milk the goats each morning, and then we would go back to the farm to sell it. It was inconvenient, but at least we knew we were safe.

Jeremy's aunt and uncle finally returned. I was glad to be done and ready to go home. Camping was getting to be a chore, even though we could go back to the farm to shower and cook.

It was a tense meeting when Aunt Rose visited the fairgrounds to check on her goats. Cocoa's injury had healed well, and she was back with the herd. The goats went nuts upon seeing Rose, and it was easy to tell they loved her dearly, gently butting their heads up against her and that sort of thing.

I had no idea what she was going to do with them, but neither I nor Jeremy thought it was a good idea to take them back home. And when Uncle Mark told us something had completely obliterated his blackberry stand, literally pulled the plants up by the roots, we were all concerned about any of them going back.

Aunt Rose ended up taking the goats to a friend's farm, one right on the edge of town, where she felt they would be safe. They had a small travel trailer, and Uncle Mark hauled it down there so she could stay overnight when she wanted to. I guess he and the dogs ended up staying there, also.

Last I heard, they had the farm up for sale. I doubt if it lasted long, as it was beautiful property. I'll never know, as Jeremy and I lost touch not long after that. We were both fired from our banking job, and he decided to take a job in New Mexico managing an RV park. I have no idea how he found it, but we ended up losing touch.

I myself moved to Salt Lake City, where I enrolled in the university to study filmmaking. I had no illusions about the job market for such a degree, but I decided that if I ever saw anything like I saw that night on the Puyallup farm, I wanted to be able to film it.

Actually, the real reason was because I'd worked hard since I was a kid and decided it was time to do something fun. I loved it and even ended up making a living at it, though filming weddings isn't really all that much fun.

In any case, I'm far away from Washington and volcanoes, goats, and, I hope, Bigfoot.

———

9

FISH AND SHIPS

I had a fun retired couple (I'll call them Cliff and Joan) sign up for one of my all-day fishing seminars in Bozeman, Montana, and they told the following story over one of my Dutch-oven dinners afterwards.

Cliff apparently ended up telling Joan all about what he saw, but neither are afraid to go out into the wilds—except they avoid Ruby Beach.

—Rusty

My name is Cliff, and I want to tell you about something that happened years ago on Ruby Beach, which is on the southwest coast of the Olympic Peninsula. My family was with me, my two girls and wife, but they didn't see what I saw, though they did see the tracks.

My girls, Julia and Renee, have long since become adults, but at the time, they were around seven and eight years old. I'm thankful they were protected from the shock I experienced. The sight will always stay with me, even though I've tried to forget it, believe me.

Ruby Beach is a really neat place in that you can explore for miles along the Pacific Coast. It's been called the most beautiful beach in Washington, partly because of its remote location. It's off Highway

101, south of where the Hoh River empties into the ocean, and north of Destruction Point.

The beach features incredible sea stacks, tangles of driftwood, and interesting sea creatures in its tide pools. It's protected by three national wildlife refuges and the Olympic Coast National Marine Sanctuary. There are also large nesting colonies of birds, like common murres and tufted puffins. In other words, even though it's frequented by people, it's still a wild and beautiful place.

Back then, and this was a good 20 years ago, as a young family, we didn't have much money. My wife, Joan, and I both worked for local schools as teachers. We both had long schedules in winter, but lots of free time in the summer, when we would spend a lot of time together as a family. I really treasure the memories we made—except for this one.

One of the things we could do together that was free was to go tide pooling on one of the nearby beaches. Ruby was our favorite, and because the coast is so rocky, it offers excellent tide pooling. It gives me the shivers to think of what was on the beach at the same time we were, though we certainly didn't know it.

Tide pools are what's left when the tide goes out, but there's actually a lot more to tide pooling than you might think. The pools are home to very diverse ecosystems, with some species at the base of the food chain while others are at the top.

Tide pools may have gobs of slippery seaweed and things like barnacles, sand dollars, sea anemones, and shells. You need to wear shoes that aren't slick and that you can get wet.

To effectively tide pool, you need to go when the tide is below two feet. You have to study the tide calendars, and if there are king tides, you just stay away, plus you have to watch for sweepers, waves that come from nowhere. Since it's in a national park, you can't take anything with you, so we would just examine what we'd find, usually trying not to touch it.

Ruby Beach is also well-known for riptides, so we never let the girls swim in the ocean there, though some of the tide pools were large enough that they could swim in them. The pools warmed up in the sun, so were much more relaxing than the cold Washington ocean waters.

The day I found the tracks, we were looking for sea stars. When the tide is out, the beach has a big sandbar that has a sea-star nursery in the water between the sandbar and the beach. A lot of sea stars have died because of a sea-star wasting sickness, so finding sea stars was always exciting.

Keep in mind that Ruby Beach has lots of rocks, which makes for great tide pooling, and it gets its name from the red rocks that are scattered all over the beach. Along with the rocks, it's also littered with weathered logs brought in by storms from nearby forests and logging activity. This makes the beach hard to get to, as you have to climb and scramble over the logs after going down a steep trail from the restroom and parking lot.

There's one place on the beach where a long tide pool forms up against a rock barrier and stretches for a long ways. I left the girls there with their mom, as it was a place we'd explored many times and was safe. I wanted to hike on down and check out the nearby sea stacks, which are like tiny islands. They sometimes have sea lions and seals resting on them, and I had my binoculars and wanted to check them out.

As I got farther from the tide pool where the rest of my family was swimming and exploring, I began to notice how peaceful and quiet it was, and I was filled with a sense of how special it was to be there and to see how beautiful the natural world could be.

One of the larger sea stacks, the one you often see in photographs, seemed to beckon me. It was called Abbey Island and was accessible only during low tide, when the sand extended out to it. During high tide, you would be stuck out there, though if you waited a few hours for the next low tide you could get back to the beach.

I was nearing Abbey Island when I spotted something in the sand —tracks! Huge tracks, very distinct, as if recently made, and they were about three times the size of my tracks and much deeper. And they had toes, as if whoever made them was barefoot.

I shivered, even though it was a beautiful sunny morning. What in the world could have made tracks like that?

Pausing and leaning on a big log, I gazed out at Abbey Island. It was big and even had trees growing on its top. I had actually been on it before, having gone there at low tide with my brother when we were teens. There were plenty of places on it where an animal could live and not be seen, especially if it stayed around on the seaward side.

Resting there on the log, I was getting ready to head back when I noted how odd it was there were no other people on the beach. But it was still fairly early in the day, and I knew people would eventually show up. Later, I wondered if anyone else had seen the tracks, though they seemed to be very recent.

To be completely honest, I knew I was kidding myself by hanging around and pretending I had no clue about the tracks, that they were just from some animal, because I knew deep inside exactly what that particular animal was—it had to be Bigfoot, or Sasquatch. I knew that native myths and legends of this area were rife with stories about this rainy coast and the strange things who lived there.

I myself had heard what could be described as monkey chatter and hair-raising howls while out hiking the many trails of the national park, mostly with my brother when we were younger. I hadn't hiked much since getting married and working full-time, but I knew the area was infamous as good Bigfoot habitat.

But I didn't want to believe in Bigfoot—no crazy stories for me, because if I believed in Bigfoot, would it be prudent to take my family into these wild places?

Growing up in Washington, I'd heard plenty of stories, but I tended to be skeptical, because I knew such stuff was easy to fake. In fact, my brother and I more than once had faked howls and wood knocks when out in the forests where we knew there were other people around. We thought it was fun, but now I'm kind of regretful to think we may have scared innocent people.

So, there on Ruby Beach, I stood both in belief and disbelief, then decided it had to be a prank. I began following the tracks, but it wasn't long before they headed right for Abbey Island along the sandy strip exposed by the low tide. I could now see a cave in the base of the island, and it looked like the tracks were headed for it.

I had no inclination to stick around, and quickly made my way back to where my wife and kids were swimming, looking for sea stars. They hadn't found any, but instead had found sea anemones, which seem to be the most common wildlife on the beach. One of the deeper tide pools had thousands of them lining the rocks in shades of greens, pinks, whites, and grays.

I tried to focus on their finding and shake off the weird feeling I now had, a feeling that things weren't what they seemed to be, and that I was being watched. Everyone else seemed normal, laughing and splashing and having fun, but I felt like we should leave, and I soon had them rounded up and heading for our car, saying I didn't feel well.

I hated to cut everyone's fun short, but something was telling me to get out of there. It was weird, because by now other people had showed up and everything seemed normal.

By the time we got a few miles down the road, I said I was feeling better, so we stopped at Kalaloch Beach and continued tide pooling. Everything felt fine, and I decided it would be wise to go there in the future instead of to Ruby.

Now what's really strange is that the next day, while sitting in my back yard watching the birds at our feeder, I felt the exact same sense that things weren't what they seemed to be, that something was off. It was the oddest feeling, and I actually looked around to see if someone was watching me.

Had something followed me home? I laughed at the thought. We didn't live close to Ruby Beach, it was a good hour's drive away, and no animal could've followed us. But the feeling was there, all the same, as illogical as it seemed.

I went inside, made some coffee, then went downstairs and watched a train video. Joan and the kids had gone shopping, and when they came home, she was surprised to find me inside on a beautiful day. I just told her I still wasn't feeling too good. I didn't want to mention the tracks and scare her.

Well, that was the last time I had that strange feeling—until we decided to go back to the beach, that is. It was my youngest daughter Julia's birthday, and everyone in the family always gets to pick what we do on their special day.

She opted for Ruby Beach, not knowing I preferred not to go there. I tried to talk her into a dozen other things—a museum visit, going to the lighthouse, even shopping—but she wanted the beach.

I decided it would be OK, though I later regretted that decision.

I checked the tide charts, and a low tide wouldn't happen until late evening, so there would be no real tide pooling. But she wanted to go anyway, so off we went to spend a day at the beach, supplied with beach chairs, picnic items, and a birthday cake. We would explore the beach and just enjoy being out.

A few people were there, most out walking their dogs, as you can let them off-leash there. We walked down the beach the opposite way of Abbey Island, looking for starfish and shells.

It wasn't long before we came to a place where someone had obviously been digging for clams or mussels, which they'd found, judging by the numerous empty shells on the beach. We wondered who would be disregarding the national park's rules.

Joan and the girls kept walking, while I lingered, looking for clues as to who had been digging. Large mounds of sand were piled all around, and there were even a few gobs of kelp all tangled in with the dirt.

It was then that I found another track. It all fell into place—the destruction wasn't human, but rather by an animal, a very large animal.

I searched for more tracks, which were hard to find in the rocks, but I finally found another, then another, then they meshed together into a trackway that led into the tumbled brush behind the beach, and I again had the feeling of being watched.

It had been a mistake coming here, and now everyone was on up the beach, with this thing between them and the car. I ran as fast as I could, following them. I had to find them and be sure we somehow avoided this stretch of beach. Maybe we could get out on the road somehow, though I knew it was a tangled mass of rainforest jungle between the beach and the highway.

We would have to go back to the trail coming down from the parking area. I soon caught up with everyone, told them I again wasn't feeling well, then tried to herd them back to the car without alarming them that something was wrong.

They had found a small octopus in a pool and didn't want to leave, but even though my wife seemed puzzled, she sensed something was going on and turned around, the girls reluctantly following.

There was one point on the beach where the vegetation came right down to the water, and as we made our way through, I was keenly aware of how vulnerable we would be if something did want to attack us.

As we hurried along, nearing the place where I'd seen the tracks going into the vegetation up the hill, I tried to reason with myself. Why the fear? I hadn't really even seen anything, and even if there was a Bigfoot nearby, there was no reason to think it would harm us. Lots of people came to the beach every day, and there had never been any reports of anything like that.

Imagine my surprise and shock when I looked back to see something large and dark standing at the edge of the forest, watching us, not more than fifty feet away. We had walked right past it!

We were nearing Cedar Creek, where the trail climbed from the beach to the parking area, and now another family was coming down, heading our way. We greeted them, and I stopped as they went by, saying something about having seen a bear up that way and that they might want to go the other direction.

They thanked me and turned around, going toward Abbey Island, as my wife asked why I hadn't told her that. This, of course, made them more eager to get back to the car.

We again ended up at Kalaloch Beach, where we celebrated Julia's birthday and then went on home.

It would be great if my story ended here, for I wouldn't have the restlessness I now face when I go outdoors. But it doesn't.

Fast forward to my wife coming home from work talking about how a coworker was out at Ruby Beach the previous day watching sea otters. Now if one has binoculars, you can spot all kinds of wildlife along the Washington coast, including whales and dolphins, but spotting sea otters can be challenging.

Because sea otters have the densest fur of any mammal, which makes great insulation, they were pretty much trapped out by fur trappers.

Sea otters are important to maintaining a balance between kelp and urchin populations, and kelp forests are important because they protect the coast by absorbing energy and making waves less severe. They are important to many creatures, including sea urchins, the otters' main food, which will multiply and devour kelp if the otters don't keep them in check.

So, sea otters from Alaska were reintroduced on the Washington coast. They're still hard to spot, but if you see kelp forests offshore, you'll probably see sea otters. And when otters appear, it makes the local grapevine, as they're so much fun to watch, bobbing and ducking in the kelp forests.

Joan was determined to take the kids out to see the sea otters, especially since Renee had done a science project in school about them. I reminded her of the so-called bear, but she was adamant, saying bears wouldn't bother a group of people.

I had no desire to go back to Ruby Beach, in fact, I was dreading the place, but I felt it was important for me to go along to make sure everyone was OK. That was probably a bit of hubris, thinking I could protect anyone from a Bigfoot. But at least I knew what was out there and what to be looking for, besides sea otters that is.

By the time everyone was ready to go, it had turned into a multi-car event, with friends and neighbors going along. This made me feel much better, for I felt there was safety in numbers.

Rumor had it the otters were near Abbey Island, so that's where the crowd headed—I counted over 22 kids and adults. The tide was going out, but the spit that ran from the beach to the island was still under water.

I had binoculars, as did everyone else, and I scanned the island, especially the cave, but saw nothing unusual. Someone said, "Over there!" and pointed to an area where little dots swam around. Looking through the binoculars, it was easy to see they were sea otters.

I watched for awhile as they ducked in and out of some kelp, seeming to be playing. But soon a groan of disbelief came from the crowd, and I could see something black and large among the otters, who were now frantically fleeing.

A huge arm flailed from the water, trying to grab one, but came back empty. I could barely make out a huge head bobbing around, then going underwater. I knew what it was, but I hoped no one else would figure it out.

"A seal's trying to catch an otter!" One of the kids exclaimed.

The otters were quickly gone, and the head also disappeared. It wasn't long before I saw a large creature slip out of the water and duck into the cave.

This time, the light was just right, and I could tell it was just a small alcove, not a cave proper, but it was deep enough to hide the creature. No one else seemed to notice, as they were all focused on the area where the sea otters had been.

We waited for the otters to come back, but knowing what they were dealing with, I knew we wouldn't see them again that day. Just as I was thinking it was time to gather my family and leave, I saw the kayakers.

Ruby Beach is very popular for sea kayakers, who like to explore the sea stacks and rocks in the area. They always wear wetsuits, as the water's cold, even in the summer.

As I watched, three kayakers came around from the back side of Abbey Island, stopping near the alcove where the Bigfoot hid. I wanted to yell at them, but there was no way they could hear me, so all I could do was watch.

They almost kayaked on by, but at the last minute, they stopped, as if wanting to explore the alcove. They beached their boats and all three got out, then went up to the dark cavity.

I held my breath, and sure enough, mere moments later, all three ran and jumped into their boats, pushing them off the shore. The dark creature was right behind them, and I could see it clearly through my binoculars.

It was horrific, like something from a bad movie, huge and hairy with a face that grimaced with hostility. I was amazed that it didn't chase the kayakers, for it looked like it was ready to kill.

And yet, it didn't harm them. Nor did it harm me when I was on the beach alone. Maybe Bigfoot really is harmless, though it will scare you to death.

It was hard to not stare at it, but it quickly went back into the alcove, as if it knew we could see it.

I could tell from the speed and direction that the kayakers would soon land where we were on the beach, and I pretty much panicked. They were sure to talk about what they'd just seen, and I didn't want my daughters or any of the other kids to know a Bigfoot was nearby. It would give them nightmares. I wasn't sure what to do.

Finally, I yelled out to everyone that I'd just received a call from a ranger, and they wanted the beach cleared as there was a bear sighting. Fortunately, everyone believed me, and they all took off for the trail back to the parking area.

I put my binoculars to my eyes just in time to see the large dark creature slip out of the alcove and into the ocean near Abbey Island. Was it coming my way?

Just about then, the kayakers arrived. They abandoned their boats on the beach while yelling frantically at me to leave, then ran along the beach to the trail going up to the parking lot.

I hightailed it up the trail also, for I knew the Bigfoot couldn't be very far away. Most everyone was gone by the time I made it up, and my family and I were soon on our way home. One of the kayakers was talking to someone on his phone, so I figured they had a ride covered, plus there were other people around.

While my family was getting into our car, I had that same feeling

I'd had when I'd first found the tracks, like something was amiss and that I was being watched.

On the way home, I vowed to never again go to Ruby Beach. I knew my family would want to know why I felt that way, and I struggled with whether or not I should tell them Bigfoot is real, as much as I wish it wasn't.

I finally decided to let it be. There was no need to make them worry or be afraid, as the creature hadn't harmed anyone, as fierce as it looked. It wasn't too long after that it became a moot point, as we both decided it would be nice to try someplace new and accepted jobs in the desert town of Tucson.

My girls grew up and now have their own families, both having moved back to the Pacific Northwest. Joan and I retired in Tacoma, so we've come full circle, as we wanted to be near our grandkids. And when they ask us to take them to the beach I usually do, but we don't go to Ruby.

———

10

THE TOTEM POLE

I met Joey while walking the beach on Whidbey Island while my wife Sarah was at a nearby geology seminar. We'd come from Colorado just the day before, and I was on my own, exploring, which I love to do.

Joey was sitting on a large rock and greeted me as I walked by. He seemed to be a local from the fishing equipment he was carrying, and I was curious as to what kind of fish he was catching.

We ended up spending several hours together, fellow fishermen, caught up in fishing stories. We eventually got around to talking about the history of the area, as I didn't know much about Washington and was eager to learn more.

Come to find out, he was a native in the real use of the term, as in indigenous, and he had some interesting things to tell me about the native tribes in the area. This story was a bonus, not one I ever expected to hear, but in my opinion, definitely worth retelling.

—Rusty

. . .

My name is Joey, and if I mentioned my last name it would immediately be recognized by a number of people in the Seattle area, so I'd best stay incognito. I'm a member of the Tlingit Tribe, and I'm originally from Juneau, Alaska, but I married into the Nooksack Tribe here in Washington. Since it's such a small tribe, lots of people would know who I am since I'm very active in community affairs.

Most of the people I know and work with are aware that there are historical tribal Sasquatch stories, but I prefer to not get involved with the subject matter as it does cause some contention.

There are tribal members who feel that advertising a belief in Sasquatch results in Sasquatch researchers invading our private space. We've had such people want to interview tribal members, as well as to come onto tribal lands. The irony is that the Nooksack weren't a recognized Indian tribe for a long time and thereby don't have a reservation.

But the Tlingit have a lot of land, though most of it's in Alaska. There is a big Tlingit community in Seattle, as well as in San Francisco, but the major communities are more in Skagway, Haines, Ketchikan, Wrangell, and Sitka.

The Tlingit are famous for their amazing totem poles and intricate wood carvings. Most of our communities are situated in incredible landscapes, bordering the wilds, and many of us still practice traditional hunting and gathering, which means we're outdoors a lot.

This event took place in Washington, though it was almost in Canada, being really close to the border. Let's just say it's a small village that has almost died out but has some of the most incredible totem poles you'll ever see.

The totem pole is a work of art, and the craftsman who carve them are held in high regard by their communities. Local trees are used, and the woodworkers prefer alder and red cedar trees as their material. Alder is soft and easy to work with, especially with hot stones, which carvers use to burn designs into the wood before it's chiseled into its final form.

The poles usually showcase animals, family crests, and spiritual symbols. They tell important stories and legends, as well as showing a family's social status. Totem poles are often mistaken to be religious in nature, but that's not the case. Animals are important in the history and legends of most Northwest natives, with specific meanings. We believe that the spirits of these animals will help you when you need it.

One example of this is the orca, a common sight along the Pacific Northwest and the coast of Alaska that, to the native people, symbolizes strength, power, and protection.

These beliefs about animals play into the story I'm about to tell, because the animal featured on the totem pole in this case was not one anybody wanted help from.

Another thing to be aware of is that the phrase "low on the totem pole," which is used to designate someone of low status, does not reflect how the totem pole is actually arranged. In reality, the closer you are to the bottom of the pole, the higher ranking you are as a member of the community.

OK, enough background, on with the story. This happened not very long ago, so you can rest assured Sasquatch is alive and well, at least in the Pacific Northwest along the Canada border. The people in this story are my relatives, which means I have the right to tell the story, as only clan members can tell the stories of their clans. Since the native people didn't have a written language, everything was told through story, and we often would use the totem poles to help tell it, as they represent our history.

My grandparents live on the very edge of the village, with large trees wrapping their house with the wonderful smell of cedar. My grandfather had always wanted to cut some of the trees down so more light came into the house, but my grandmother wouldn't let him, saying the spirits of the trees would protect them.

Our clan had once lived in a longhouse, made of wood and cedar bark, with each family having its own area for cooking and sleeping, but with the passage of time and people coming and going more, we finally built a sort of plank house for just our family, and eventually my grandparents lived in it, the rest of us moving to the city for jobs and such.

I guess my grandmother started to feel bad for my grandfather, as she told him he could cut down four of the biggest trees if he would agree to have them made into totem poles. This would not be cheap, because carvers can pretty much charge whatever they want.

My grandfather decided this was a good trade, and he promptly had the four biggest trees next to the house cut down, which really opened things up. He then had the trees trimmed and hauled to the carver, who was just on the other side of the village.

It takes a long time to carve a totem pole, but finally one was ready. They got it to my grandparents' house, where it would serve as a property corner marker, which is another purpose the poles are used for. The entire village helped erect it, with a picnic celebration. It sat on the edge of a small valley that was the boundary of our clan property, off the main path.

OK, remember where I said the lower on the totem pole the higher the honor? Well, the pole had our family crest at the top, and then plenty of animals, including raven, salmon, deer, and an orca, but at the bottom was a large furry creature that everyone thought must be a bear.

I remember looking at it closely and thinking that there's no way it was a bear. I even asked my grandmother about it in she said no it's not a bear. Apparently she had asked the carver to put a picture of a Sasquatch on it. When I asked her why, she said because Sasquatch had been coming to the property for many years and she wanted to honor them. I got the feeling that she was afraid of them and thought this kind of honor would keep them from harming anything.

Did our people believe in Bigfoot? Yes, though we didn't call it that. There were a number of names for it, including Big Brother and Fast Walker. Bigfoot is also known as Sasquatch, from Sasq'ets, called that by First Nations peoples in southwestern British Columbia.

The term Sasquatch gradually came into use in our village, but by then very few people had heard of or seen a Sasquatch and it seems as if they were disappearing, possibly moving further north into

British Columbia as more and more people moved into the Pacific Northwest.

Keep in mind that the Klondike gold rush in the late 1800s brought 100,000 permanent residents to Seattle and this of course trickled down into villages in the nearby countryside.

I never felt comfortable going out to where the totem pole sat. It always felt like I was intruding on someone else's land or home. Did I ever see a Sasquatch? No, nor did I ever hear one. But my grandfather did.

He was sitting in their living room one evening, reading something or other, when he heard a loud howl outside. It seems that my grandmother was gone. He opened the front door and listened and the howling seemed to be coming from just down the road a little bit. It really scared him and he locked the door and made sure all the windows were closed.

My grandfather is pretty much in tune with the natural world and is actually about as close to what some tribes call a medicine man as you could get, but he still felt an indescribable fear.

When he told my grandmother about it, she freaked out and immediately called the carver and ordered the other three poles. These were expensive, and she ended up borrowing the money from my dad, who worked in Seattle in construction.

He wasn't real happy about it, but he said she was so scared that he couldn't turn her down. She thought the other three totem poles with Sasquatch on them would protect them. She didn't invite the village when they were raised, and just had a private ceremony with the family.

Well nothing more happened, but one day I went out to the first pole and noticed that something had been chewing on it. I assumed it was a bear or something, but the only part chewed on was the Sasquatch. I decided it was because it was at the bottom and easy to access.

At this point, people started having Sasquatch encounters in the forest around the village. Where no one had even remembered they existed, they were now seeing them and being followed and harassed by them.

Grandma had her work cut out explaining to the townspeople why there hadn't been a Sasquatch encounter for many decades and now it was happening at least once or twice a week. People were terrified and blamed the totem poles, saying the carvings had drawn them in.

Grandpa was now afraid to even go walking on his own property. This was not good, because he was getting old and needed daily exercise. I tried to encourage him to go walking in town, but he wouldn't do it. I've never seen my grandfather afraid before or since, so this gave me pause.

Finally, my dad bought him a tricycle, one of those adult ones that you can ride and it has a little place behind the seat where you can carry things. Grandpa would keep it at my aunt's house in town and Grandma would drive him there, and he'd then go for rides.

Grandma got out every day because she worked with our small senior center cooking meals. Sometimes Grandpa would go in and have lunch with her.

Well, one day I went to visit and went out to the original totem pole and found the Sasquatch had been almost completely destroyed. It looked like someone had taken a sharp stick and just gouged it out. It really bothered me, as I thought the townspeople were doing it because they thought it was attracting Sasquatch.

I then walked around the property to the other three poles and found basically the same thing, that the Sasquatch part was being destroyed. I told Grandma about it, and she was even more upset. She thought that it was townspeople who didn't like Sasquatch and wanted to dissuade it from coming around.

My grandmother is not a passive person, and once she gets riled up she's pretty hard to stop. It was her idea to put game cameras on the totem poles. That way we could see what was going on. I had the privilege of mounting them on trees near the poles, and I tried to place them where they weren't very conspicuous.

I went back after several nights and checked them, and there was nothing except an occasional deer and a couple of foxes. We kind of forgot about the cameras until a few weeks later.

Well, one evening, Grandpa and Grandma heard a screaming from out in the forest. It came closer and closer to the house, to where it seemed it was just outside. This was truly terrifying to them, and they called me and tried to have me listen to it through the phone, but it didn't come through, though the fact that they were scared did.

I drove out there and tried to calm them down, telling them they could come spend the night at our house, which both decided was a good idea. We gathered up their stuff and left, and the next day when we came back I went out to the totem poles to check the game cameras. I was chilled, to say the least.

First. let me say that an average totem pole can weigh a ton or more. That's over 2,000 pounds. It would take an incredibly strong group of people to take one down, unless you had some kind of heavy equipment, like a skidsteer or backhoe.

The first pole I visited had been wrenched from the ground, pulled straight up, then toppled. Have you ever gone to the Highland Games where they do this thing called tossing the caber? It's a contest to see how far one can throw a small telephone pole. The men are incredibly strong and still have trouble with a small pole, which weighs around 150 pounds.

Whatever had pulled the totem pole from the ground had help, though, for I found all kinds of tracks around the area, and all were huge. And the lower part of the pole had been completely destroyed to the point where there was nothing left depicting a Sasquatch.

I went to the tree where I'd placed a game camera, but it was gone, with more nearby tracks.

Now I was beginning to feel spooked, like something was watching me, and the hair on my arms and neck stood straight up. A very distinct thought entered my mind—you are not welcome here, go away.

I didn't fight it, but instead took off running. As I ran, I thought I could hear footsteps paralleling me in the bushes, but I couldn't see anything. But a totally illogical terror hit me—I say illogical because it was like someone was trying to kill me, and yet there was nothing there. I was quickly back at my grandparents'.

When they saw how terrified I was, they asked if I'd gone to the other poles, and I said no. We all talked about it, and we decided we'd made the Sasquatch angry by putting up a depiction of them on the poles.

We needed to get all the poles out of there as soon as we could, which would involve again hiring the guy who had the skidsteer and had helped us set them. The problem was, he wanted nothing to do with it, having heard the howls himself from the village.

The next day, I got my brother to go with me out to the other poles, and we were both armed with shotguns. I wasn't surprised to find the poles down, just like the first one, and the game cameras gone. We both felt an ominous presence while there and didn't stick around long.

Now my grandmother was fit to be tied. As stubborn as she was, she didn't want the poles around any longer, yet we couldn't find anyone who would go retrieve what was left of them. Totem poles were meant to eventually decay back into the earth, but she wanted these gone, not out there making the Sasquatch angry.

To say she was the town pariah right then would be an understatement, for everyone knew she'd erected totem poles with Sasquatch carvings at the same time the Sasquatch started harassing everyone. No one had been injured yet, but several had close calls from having large limbs and rocks thrown at them.

She decided we should go out and burn them. This was sacrilege —you didn't just go out and burn totem poles. I told her she would probably be even more of a pariah if she did that, so she then decided we should bury them.

Our grandfather talked her out of that, especially since it would mean burying our family crest, which had ravens on it, as well as the rest of what was actually a woodcarver's work of art. We knew the artists would be angry and insulted. So what to do?

My brother finally came up with what we considered a good solution—we would cut off the bottom of the pole with the mangled Sasquatch carvings, bury those, then haul the pole to the house and erect them in the yard. It would be better for everyone to see them that way, anyway.

My brother and I took chain saws out to the poles and cut the bottoms off, then we rented a skidsteer and dragged the poles up to the house, where we had friends help us erect them. I will say they looked pretty impressive there, and we've enjoyed seeing them.

Since we had the skidsteer for one more day, we decided it would be a good time to go bury the Sasquatch carvings. They had only been out there for a couple of days, mind you, waiting for us to go bury them, but when we got out there, they were gone. Nary a trace was left. And yes, more big tracks, but no sense of anything being there watching us. It felt very peaceful.

That was the end of the Sasquatch visitations around the village. There are things about this event that puzzle me, mainly, how did the Sasquatch know about the poles in the first place, since no one had seen them coming around? My grandpa says they're there, we just don't know it, as they're night creatures and very secretive.

We're all kind of upset that the game cameras went missing, but in hindsight, maybe it was a good thing, for who really wants to see what we were dealing with? If sensing it nearby was so terrifying, what would actually seeing one do to a person?

So, that's the story, and since you're not in my clan, Rusty, you technically can't tell it to anyone without my permission, as you can only tell stories about your own clan. But given what happened and that I believe others should know that Sasquatch is a real being and can harm you, I think it's important for you to tell this story, and I give you my clan's full permission.

11

BIGFOOT, MEET EARTHWORM

I wasn't sure why Bob had joined one of my flyfishing trips in the Colorado Rockies as he was a local and could easily find out where the best fishing spots were, but he told me he was interested in learning the sport, as he'd never fished in his entire life, even though his dad had been a fisherman.

He later told me that he and his dad had butted heads a lot, so he'd never followed in his footsteps, though when he told this story, he realized he had more than he'd realized by working for the railroad. Whether his dad ever saw a Bigfoot is a story we'll never know, as he had passed away a few years earlier.

Bob told this story over dinner around a campfire, and I have to agree with what his wife had said about him being a good storyteller. It was engaging from start to finish.

—Rusty

Rusty, I work for the railroad, but I'd prefer not to say exactly what I do, but you can guess I'm either a conductor or engineer, since I get to ride in the big engines.

When this happened, I worked for the BNSF, the Burlington Northern Santa Fe, as that's easy to guess when I tell you where all this happened—on what's called the Lakeside Subdivision, which consists of track running the 150 miles from Pasco to Spokane, Washington. Trains call certain sections of track subdivisions, and the BNSF owns that stretch.

The eastern part of the Evergreen State is mostly rolling hills, not exactly where one would expect to see a Bigfoot. Oh, and according to my supervisor at the time, I didn't see a Bigfoot and wasn't supposed to tell anyone I did. He said I would lose my job, but my job was union, so that was unlikely. I did keep it to myself, no point in poking the bear, but I don't work there anymore.

I'll add here that when I did tell this story to one of my coworkers, he said he knew a fellow who'd seen a Bigfoot crossing the Latah Creek Bridge right out of Spokane. That bridge is 175 feet tall and over 1,000 feet long, and I bet that Bigfoot got a thrill. He said there were people stopped on I-90 watching it. I dunno about that story, but who knows? People don't believe my story, either.

I've worked on western railroads all my life, in fact, my grandfather helped build the Moffat Tunnel right here in Colorado, and my dad worked for Union Pacific. I now work for Union Pacific running the Moffat Tunnel Subdivision, so I've kind of followed in my grandpa and dad's footsteps.

I've seen some beautiful stretches of rail, but the Lakeside Sub isn't one of them. It's just the same thing over and over, rolling hills and wheat fields, until you come to Marshall Canyon, at least, and that's where things get interesting, and they got *real* interesting one particular day. The Lakeside Sub does go through some stands of pines, but it's not real forest until you get to Marshall Canyon.

I'll add that BNSF's Lakeside Sub sees 50 trains each day—coal, grain, potash, mixed manifest, intermodal—so I know there are other railroaders who have seen this thing or one like it. It has to live in the forest there, and there has to be more than one for it to reproduce.

Or maybe the ones I saw were outliers, lost or just traveling through, because I sure don't see that sub as being Bigfoot country. I could see one living near Pasco along the Columbia River, as there's more wild country available to them there.

I wish I'd known to ask my grandfather and dad if they'd ever seen anything like a Bigfoot. As many miles as they covered in trains through wild country, it seems likely, but I'll never know. When I try to ask fellow railroad employees, they either laugh or look at me like I'm nuts, except for the guy who mentioned the Latah Creek Bridge.

What would be *really* interesting is talking to Lewis and Clark. They traversed all this country when things were really wild—or better still, to ask the natives who lived here before any whites came into the country. People say they had legends about Bigfoot, but I've never heard or read any.

The day that I had this weird experience, I was on a grain train, what rail fans call an "earthworm." BNSF has around 100 covered hopper cars that resemble earthworms when they're rolling down the rails. You see them most often at grain elevators.

Anyway, we would get off in Spokane, switching with another crew who would take it on its way to an export terminal some-where on the West Coast. But that day was the last in a series of odd days which started months before. I didn't realize what I was possibly seeing until I actually saw it in its entirety, but I will say it left me feeling odd and out of sorts on the days I experienced its presence.

It feels weird to say the word presence, but I don't know how else to describe it. I could always feel a presence as the train rolled through a certain part of Marshall Canyon, a feeling that ended after I saw the creature. I think it must've left the area after that, because I never sensed anything.

How do you feel a presence? I can't describe it, it's just that you feel like you're being watched. How can you feel like you're being watched while rolling through the countryside on a train? Well, the trains slow down for certain sections of the canyon, and that's where I felt it, but I will admit it seems impossible and this is where most people stop believing my story.

The place I'm thinking of is a deep cut in the basalt, a place where the train is actually lower than the cut banks. I've always felt like it would be a good place for a hobo to jump onto a train, but the truth is, they probably wouldn't make it unless the train was practically stopped.

It was a cold winter day, I'm not sure what month, but I want to say January, when we came through this cut and I suddenly got the feeling something was out there, watching us, something that maybe shouldn't be there, or maybe shouldn't even logically exist.

Now, Marshall Canyon has plenty of places for a Bigfoot to hide, and there's abundant water, with Fish Lake right there and also Minnie Creek, but it's also almost in Spokane, and there are houses and people nearby. It's not like some remote canyon deep in the Rockies. It has two rail lines running through it and a hiking trail.

So to feel like I did was kind of odd, until you look at a map and realize you're not all that far from the Turnbull National Wildlife Refuge and lots of scabland with a gazillion small lakes. But still, it wasn't like those times your imagination conjures things up when you're out in the backcountry.

I remember asking my co-worker if he felt anything, and when he said no, I laughed and said it was my overactive imagination. He wanted to know more, but I didn't want to talk about it, though I don't know why. I guess because I didn't want him to think I was losing my mind.

Well, the second time was a month or so later when we were on a westbound BNSF mixed manifest, approaching Overlook Siding. I remember the engines—we were running two SD40-2's and a SD50.

Actually, Rusty, telling this again has made me think of something —maybe the reason I felt strange was that I caught a glimpse of the Bigfoot out of the corner of my eye. My brain saw it, but my mind didn't.

I'm thinking this because the next time I felt that way I did see something—it wasn't out of the corner of my eye, but it almost was. We were approaching Overlook Siding when I thought I saw something slip into the forest.

Now, we see all kinds of wildlife on trains, and sadly enough, sometimes even run over things, but this wasn't anything normal. It was big and black and on two legs and I recall thinking for a moment that someone was out there, but it slipped away so quickly I wasn't even sure I'd seen anything. It was puzzling.

I didn't think any more about it, as I was busy with train stuff. I decided it was someone's loose bull.

Have you ever stood by a train as it goes by at a high speed? It's a noisy son of a gun, no doubt, but what's interesting is the kinds of noises it makes. Better still, stand near a tunnel as a train goes through where the sounds are amplified, or in a canyon, where the sounds echo back and forth.

It can get downright eerie. The wheels groan and squeal, the engines grind and whirr, the couplings rattle, the dynamic brakes make a sharp whine that will wake the dead, and the air compressor motors make a whoop whoop noise. Sometimes, when I was a kid, I would stay out late by the tracks and listen as the trains went by. I could hear voices that sounded like strange beings talking. It would scare me into going home.

But what's even stranger is how you can't hear a train coming until it's right on you. This is because all the noise is funneled out the sides because of the speed and how trains are long and narrow. This will come into play later.

OK, another time in Marshall Canyon, I heard those noises again, but this time, I was inside the cab of the locomotive. You certainly can hear the train there, but it's not that echoing sound you get when outside the train itself.

So imagine my surprise when I heard what sounded like voices talking, deep and off and on, but not forming words that I could understand. I thought it was the train, but when I looked out the window, I again saw something black slip into the trees, except this time, there were several, and I caught a better glimpse. I told my partner someone was cosplaying out in the forest, you know, when people dress up and act like characters from some movie or book?

He asked what they were cosplaying as, and I said maybe Bigfoot. He thought it was funny and nothing more was said, though it left me again with that strange feeling. I was getting to where I would just hold my breath until we got through Marshall Canyon, on into

Spokane or the little town of Marshall on the other end. I was developing a sort of phobia about the place.

One evening, as if to make things worse, I decided to research Bigfoot to see if that could possibly be what I was dealing with. This was before the Internet, and it was hard to get information about anything. It all quickly fizzled out, as I realized asking locals in Spokane or Marshall if they'd ever heard of Bigfoot was a good way to make people think I was nuts.

I say researching made things worse because the more I thought about it, the more convinced I was that I hadn't seen a bull or people, but something else. I wasn't convinced it was Bigfoot, because I'd never seen one to compare it to, or so was my logic. Nor did I know anyone who had seen one, except for the guy who saw one on the bridge, and he had a reputation for telling tall tales. But I knew it was something different I'd seen, whatever it was.

A couple of years passed, and I found myself still on the Lakewood Subdivision. I badly wanted to see some new country, so I'd put in for a transfer, but I never got it, so I eventually ended up quitting and getting a job with a different railroad.

But I hadn't quit yet, and it was autumn. I later wondered if these things don't maybe migrate to get away from the cold country, because that would explain a few things, mostly that I had sightings over several days, then nothing. It was like they were moving through the country, heading south.

The first one I saw was again more of a shadow, just something quickly running across the tracks in the twilight, not real definitive, but that odd feeling told me it wasn't a deer or anything else. I was surprised, because I'd kind of forgotten about seeing anything earlier, probably my brain trying to protect itself.

The second time was just a couple of days later, and this time my co-worker also saw it. It was definitely something on two legs, and it crossed the tracks in just a couple of strides and was gone. He looked at me kind of funny, as if remembering the other times I'd told him I'd seen something, but neither of us said a word.

The next time was the time that made me want to quit, which I did when I realized I wasn't going to get a transfer. My coworker didn't see a thing, and at first I was resentful of this, as I wanted someone else to have seen it so I knew I wasn't hallucinating, but I finally decided it was a good thing, for his sake.

We were close to that same cut when I, sure enough, felt that presence, then saw something up ahead on top of the bank. I could basically see only the legs, but I could tell there were several, and I knew instantly what they were—the same thing I'd been seeing off and on, but now they were much closer, just right above the tracks.

The train was going fairly slow, as it was pulling that grade with a full load, and I watched, hoping and praying these things would just stay up on the bank and not try to cross. Even though we were going slow, it can be deceptive as to how fast a train is really going and how much time you have to cross ahead of it.

Now, train fatalities are one of the things that engineers and conductors don't like to discuss. A derailment can result in injuries and/or deaths, and there are always bad things happening at railroad crossings from people who think they can outrun a train, both on foot or in vehicles. And of course, there are fatalities from what the train calls trespassers, usually hobos.

I've never been involved in a human fatality, but I have been on trains that have hit a deer or large bird. It always gives you a sinking feeling, but you can't stop a big heavy train on a dime, so you just keep going. I mean, a long heavy train can take a few miles to stop.

So when I saw these things, I held my breath. "Just stay up there," I said to myself. "Don't move." I touched the horn so they could hear us coming. Like I said, it's amazing how quiet an oncoming train can be, and there have been lots of people killed because they were on the tracks and didn't hear the train behind them.

I'll always wonder if that horn isn't what made them jump, maybe startling them. You can guess what happened next—I saw a jumble of legs and torsos and black hair come down off the side of that cut right onto the tracks in front of the train.

There wasn't time to do anything but watch as several large animals tried frantically to cross the tracks in front of the oncoming train. I say animals, but you know what they were. To this day, I have trouble saying the word Bigfoot. It's kind of like I'd rather not recognize it exists by naming it.

As the train was upon them, I could see that one was a youngster. It was just as ugly as the others, but in a cute way, if that makes any sense. And don't ask me to describe them. I'll just say all the descriptions you hear are right, they're big and hairy and ugly with faces that look like an ape married a human.

I felt bad about what was going to happen in the next brief second, but there was nothing I could do except hope they were fast enough to get on over the tracks. The mind works in weird ways, because I thought how strange it was for an earthworm to hit a Bigfoot—I was, of course, thinking of what rail fans call these big grain trains.

They made it across, except for one, and I remember the sound of hitting it—it was like hitting a big bull, and it probably weighed about the same. I did manage to see the youngster running through the trees, so I knew it had crossed safely, and I think we only hit one. Did we kill it? Probably, as it sounded like we'd hit something dead on.

My coworker was watching all this, and then he asked what we'd hit, and I said a deer. He said it must've been a big buck, and I just nodded in agreement. What we'd seen wasn't a big buck, and in my mind, it contradicted everything I knew about what existed in Washington State. I let him stay in denial, even though his eyes told him the truth.

Seeing something like that will mess with your sense of what's real, because it doesn't seem like it could be real, and yet, you know what you saw. Don't expect anyone to believe you, and I never did get to where I wanted to talk about it. It feels like something you want to forget and talking about it just brings it back. I did examine the locomotive next time we stopped, but found nothing, and there was nothing along the tracks next time we went that way.

I don't mind telling you this story, Rusty, because I know you'll believe me, but so far, nobody else has, not even my wife. She just laughed and poked me in the ribs saying I was sure a good storyteller, but not to ever tell that one to the kids, as it would scare them to death.

So I never have. Like I said, I ended up getting a different job, and boy was my wife upset when we ended up having to move and leave all her friends. But we ended up here in Colorado, and I now work for Union Pacific, and she was happy because it worked out that we ended up moving closer to her family.

I have yet to see any strange animals in these parts, unless you want to talk about all the rail fans that hang out at the Moffat Tunnel, but they're lots better looking than the critters in Marshall Canyon, that's for sure.

———

12

HANGING AROUND THE CAMPFIRE

The following story is the only one in this collection that's not new, and it comes from my first book, "Rusty Wilson's Bigfoot Campfire Stories." I've included it because it seems like a fitting conclusion to this book, as well as taking place in Washington.

Sitting around a campfire deep in the backcountry, a story like the following told by a fellow named Brian gives you the chills. This was one of those nights when we all just sat around the fire until we started nodding off, too scared to go to our tents.

—Rusty

This happened to me and some friends about five years ago, in a national park in Washington. The park has a backcountry permit system—you can't camp without a permit, and we had to apply for this way ahead of time.

We thought we'd see lots of people, as it's a popular park, but we saw almost no one the entire time we were there.

At the time, I worked for a high-tech company in Seattle. A group of us decided to go backpacking together. We were all pretty avid outdoorsmen, some were hikers and a couple of the guys were serious climbers. We were all seasoned and experienced outdoorsmen. There were seven of us, all told.

So, we finally got the permit and made our plans and were soon camped in a high alpine basin deep within the park. I'd rather not say exactly where this happened.

It took us a good hard day to get in there, carrying all our gear on our backs. We were tired, and after we set up camp, we built a fire and cooked dinner.

It was soon dark, as it had taken quite awhile to set everything up. We had a great spaghetti dinner and were soon all crashed out in our tents, exhausted.

I'll add that I was the only one with any kind of weapon. I had a large Bowie knife, and I slept with it under my pillow. I'd had a run-in with a black bear in Yellowstone and always carried that knife. The bear hadn't harmed me, just scared me trying to get into my tent, but I hadn't had any defense at all, so thus the knife on this trip. This was before you were allowed to carry guns in national parks.

I guessed it to be about 3 a.m. when I woke. I just lay there. Something had awakened me, but I didn't know what. Then I heard some scuffling noise and some low talking. I crawled out of my tent and found several of the guys up and talking in a whisper.

I didn't even have time to ask, when I heard it. From way off in the distance, I mean several miles away, we could hear a sound that, for lack of better description, sounded like an air-raid siren. It was the weirdest thing you can imagine, being way up there in the wilderness, to hear a siren.

But what was even weirder, and what left me with a knot in the pit of my stomach, was the fact that the noise was moving, was gradually getting closer. And whatever was making it had lungs like a freight train, if a train had lungs. Whatever it was had a huge set of lungs, it sounded miles away and yet was so distinct. It really filled the air, it had vibrations to it.

By now the rest of the guys were up, and everyone looked concerned. It was a unique situation for all of us.

And remember, I was the only one armed, and not very well, at that. A Bowie knife isn't really much of a weapon in a deal like that.

We kind of ended up bunched together, and someone said we should build a fire. So we ended up grabbing some wood from the forest around us, and put it with the bit of wood from our earlier fire.

We built a fire, and some of the guys continued to gather wood, but no one would get far from camp. We used our headlamps, and it was kind of eerie seeing all the lights nervously moving around the forest while that noise just got closer and closer.

By the time it was near us, it actually shook the forest. It was the most intense sound I've ever heard, and it brought shivers to the back of my neck, literally.

Before long it was really close to our camp, and it was so loud it made my ears ring, you could actually feel the sound waves going through the air.

It was just this intense siren sound, it would go from low pitch to high and drop back down again. Everyone stood with their backs to the fire, and we all had big sticks, except for me, and I had my knife in my hand.

When the creature got to the edge of our camp, it just went crazy. It stopped making the siren sound and started with a high-pitched screaming, then it would stop and growl, then go back to the screaming.

That growl was absolutely terrifying, it was deep and throaty and mean sounding. We were all scared to death.

Nobody said a word. We all stood there, white as ghosts. Once in awhile the fire would kind of die down and someone would grab some wood from the pile and get it going again. This seemed to enrage the creature, and it would start screaming again.

It then began circling our camp, and we could hear it breaking through the bushes and trees. It had to be large.

I swear, I was so scared I don't remember much except praying and standing there with that big knife held out in front of me.

The creature circled and circled. It knocked down several fairly large trees, a good eight inches in diameter, and one of those nearly fell on us.

We just continued to stand there in a pitiful circle around the fire. I worried that we would run out of wood, and sure enough, it was about 5 a.m., and the last bit of wood was burning.

I said to one of the guys that we needed a plan for when the wood ran out. The creature was still circling our camp. It had settled down some and wasn't screaming any more, but from the way it was breaking trees left and right, it still seemed very angry.

Once in awhile, it would lob a small tree at us—trees too green to burn, and you could see the roots. It had ripped them from the ground.

So, we made a plan, though it wasn't much of one. We hadn't had our headlights turned on, as we wanted to conserve the batteries. We decided that when the fire was dead, we'd all turn on our lights and shine it at wherever the creature was, and keep shining the lights until dawn.

We knew we could last because we all had fresh batteries, the trip having just started. If the creature wasn't afraid of our lights, well, who knows then?

So the fire died out, and we turned on our headlamps and shone them at the creature as it circled the camp. I was amazed at the energy it had, it hadn't slowed down at all.

This wasn't much of a plan, but it was all we had. If it tried to attack, we agreed to light some sticks on fire, we'd go down fighting. A kind of pitiful plan, really.

When we turned on our lights and shone them into the woods, the creature stopped short. We could now see a pair of glowing red eyes looking at us, and the eyes were a good eight feet off the ground. This scared the you-know-what out of me.

And the eyes had no flicker to them. We hadn't seen any red eyes before, it was like it had just turned them on at will.

It stood there, eyes glowing, just out of the circle of our lights, then just disappeared.

The quiet, the silence, its disappearance, were all really scary because we had no idea what was going on. Was it sneaking up on us? The uncertainty factor was really chilling.

If I tried to describe the fear of that night in detail, it would be a mixture of hopelessness, chilling terror, and astonishment.

Finally, I could see the first light of dawn as the sky to the east began to turn a pale blue. It was still a good hour before it was really light enough to see much, and by then we had all pretty much collapsed around the cold fire ring.

The night had taken its toll on us all, but not one of us went to sleep sitting there, we just sat in shock.

As soon as it was light enough to see, everyone got up and began breaking camp. There was no discussion about it, it just happened. Everyone was exhausted, but we put on our packs and headed back the way we'd come in.

It was only a few hours later when we got to the trail-head and our cars. Going downhill and pushed by fear, we got out really fast.

At that point, the sun was bright and the night seemed like a weird dream. We sat down on some rocks and began talking for the first time. I made some coffee, and someone else broke out some granola bars and cheese, and we ate like famished men, which we were.

No one had any idea what to make of any of this except one guy who had been raised in the Northwest, and he said he knew what it was. He said it was a Bigfoot, and a very angry one, probably because we had invaded its territory.

Would it have harmed us? Yes, he was sure of it, as angry as it was, it wasn't bluffing.

After a bit of talking about all this, we left and went to our respective homes. I don't think any of us has been back in the park since then. I know I've given up camping completely and have no desire to be out in the woods.

I still have an interest in the park and read the news about that area, and strangely enough, several hikers have disappeared in that part of the park since then.

A couple of years later, I took it upon myself to contact a park ranger and tell her of our experience that night.

She was very quiet, then told me what she was going to say was strictly off the record, but that the park service had quit issuing permits for that section of the park and knew something strange was afoot.

They weren't sure how to address the situation. Strange tracks had been found, and she, herself, had something black and huge stalk her while on patrol not too far from where our camp had been.

She won't go into that area alone, and the park service has now prohibited anyone from going in there at all. She told me they've had two rangers transfer and a couple of seasonals quit, and she was trying to transfer also.

I told her I understood how she feels. I myself have no desire to ever go there again.

———

ABOUT THE AUTHOR

Rusty Wilson is a fly-fishing guide based in Colorado and Montana. He's well-known for his Dutch-oven cookouts and campfires, where he's heard some pretty wild stories about the creatures in the woods, especially Bigfoot.

Whether you're a Bigfoot believer or not, we hope you enjoyed this book, and we know you'll enjoy Rusty's many others, the first of which is *Rusty Wilson's Bigfoot Campfire Stories.* Also check out Rusty's bestselling *Yellowstone Bigfoot Campfire Stories,* as well as *Bigfoot: The Dark Side, The Creature of Lituya Bay,* and *Chasing After Bigfoot: My Search for North America's Most Elusive Creature.*

Rusty's books come in ebook format, as well as in print and audio.

You'll also enjoy the first book in the Bud Shumway mystery series, a Bigfoot mystery, *The Ghost Rock Cafe.*

Other offerings from Yellow Cat Publishing include an RV series by RV expert Sunny Skye, which includes *Living the Simple RV Life.* And don't forget to check out the books by Sunny's friend, Bob Davidson: *On the Road with Joe,* and *Any Road, USA.* And finally, you'll love Roger Dean Miller's comedy thriller, *Bombing Hoffman.*